D0438387

It Was
FOOD Vs. ME
...and *I Won*

It Was
FOOD Vs. ME
... and *I Won*

Nancy Goodman

VIKING

VIKING
Published by the Penguin Group
Penguin Group (USA) Inc., 375 Hudson Street, New York, New York 10014, U.S.A.
Penguin Books Ltd, 80 Strand, London WC2R 0RL, England
Penguin Books Australia Ltd, 250 Camberwell Road, Camberwell, Victoria 3124, Australia
Penguin Books Canada Ltd, 10 Alcorn Avenue, Toronto, Ontario, Canada M4V 3B2
Penguin Books India (P) Ltd, 11 Community Centre, Panchsheel Park,
New Delhi – 110 017, India
Penguin Books (N.Z.) Ltd, Cnr Rosedale and Airborne Roads, Albany, Auckland,
New Zealand
Penguin Books (South Africa) (Pty) Ltd, 24 Sturdee Avenue, Rosebank, Johannesburg 2196,
South Africa

Penguin Books Ltd, Registered Offices: 80 Strand, London WC2R 0RL, England

First published in 2004 by Viking Penguin, a member of Penguin Group (USA) Inc.

1   3   5   7   9   10   8   6   4   2

Grateful acknowledgment is made for permission to reprint an excerpt from "Something Good" by Richard Rodgers. Copyright © 1964 by Richard Rodgers. Copyright renewed. Williamson Music owner of publication and allied rights throughout the world. International copyright secured. All rights reserved. Used by permission.

LIBRARY OF CONGRESS CATALOGING-IN-PUBLICATION DATA
Goodman, Nancy.
        It was food vs. me . . . and I won / Nancy Goodman.
        p.   cm.
        ISBN 0-670-03312-X
        1. Goodman, Nancy—Health.   2. Compulsive eaters—United States—Biography.
3. Overweight women—United States—Biography.   4. Compulsive eating—
Treatment.   I. Title.
RC552.C65G66 2004
613.2'5—dc22   2003066560

This book is printed on acid-free paper. ∞

Printed in the United States of America

To my mom, my dad, and my husband, Scott. Without you guys and all of my issues, what would a girl like me have to talk about? Thanks for all things unconditional. And to think I ever doubted your love.

To Lani, Sam, and Alex. Perfect, perfect, and perfect. When I look at you, that's what I see.

Chapter 1

It's not like the bagel was fresh. It was discarded. It wasn't sitting on a plate with garnishes of lettuce, cream cheese, or tomato. It was on the car floor. It wasn't that I had no other options, like the homeless who scrounge for any available food to survive. I had a beautiful family and a wonderful home with a kitchen full of food. Something must have been terribly wrong inside, but I didn't know what or why. All I knew was that the bagel that lay on the floor of my car, minus three bites from one of my kids, ended up getting eaten. And we had no dog.

It's not like I was unappealing, grotesque, or unhappy. I didn't look like the kind of girl who ate fuzzy bagels and cabinets of food. To the contrary, I was admired for my "discipline" and self-control. I was in great shape, cooked healthy foods, and was knowledgeable about nutrition. I knew the fat grams in fuzz. What I didn't know was why I had this curse. It was private, shameful, and painful. It was devastating and life-stealing. It was a constant in my life; I could not control my eating.

On any given day, weight gain was my fear. Weight loss was my goal. I couldn't eat a meal, couldn't eat a sandwich, and couldn't eat a bite of someone else's without worrying about losing control. And when I found myself sitting in my car after the kids had gotten out, I couldn't stop what was happening. I turned around, saw that bagel, and stuffed it into my mouth. I'll never forget that moment. I'll never forget the feeling of loss. Who was I and what was I doing? And the race to the kitchen that followed. I made a phone call that day that would forever change my life. The Bagel Day was Day One.

I'm not sure why I made the call that day. After all, I had been bingeing since my early teens. If I wasn't eating, I was thinking about eating. If I was eating, I was devastated by the inability to stop. If I was all right with my eating, I was tormented by the fear of it not lasting. Simple things like making plans were determined by my weight. I never made plans on Mondays; I would be too fat from Sunday. I needed advance notice of social plans so I could lose weight beforehand. Funerals were always a problem because they came without proper notice; I might have to be seen on a Monday. Cancellations were a necessary tool for the times I felt too fat to go.

I had many fears in my life. I was afraid of my husband's family; they had food everywhere on Sundays. I was afraid of my relatives' homes. They had cabinets and foods I knew I wouldn't be able to get away from. My friends' houses had cookies and chips that I intentionally kept out of my own home but always feared in theirs. Even my grandmother's house was scary. Parties and dinners were overwhelming. Holidays were useless. Birthdays had cake and goody bags. There were paper plates with pizza crusts, abandoned as kids left to play.

Every event, every home, every night, every day, I was never safe from food. It would be there waiting and there was nothing I could do. I would prepare myself by setting rules. I looked to my husband to help me enforce them. If I knew I was headed for trouble with food, I would ask him to watch and stand guard. "Don't let me eat," I would say. I would tell myself to be strong and strategize a plan. Maybe I would eat before I went so that I wouldn't eat as much there. Or not eat all day so I would *only* eat there. But all of my efforts would fail. No matter what I did, how hard I tried, nothing ever worked. It would win. It always did. Sometimes I went home and cried.

There was only one place I felt safe in my life and that was on a diet. A diet to me was like a big iron gate that kept food on the other side. I had no choices facing me, no points of decision that might be wrong or might lead me to bad places with eating. A diet was hope. It was success. It was the only way I could live calmly. That wonderful calm would last only awhile. Following it were the inevitable "cheats" sabotaging what success I had.

At the time I viewed those cheats as my own inability to succeed in my goal to be thin. Since small cheats led to larger cheats, which led to lost pounds gained back, I thought I was ruining my own happiness. I looked at my life. It was everything I had ever wished for. What a shame all that was ruined by one horrible problem with food. What would cure me? What would allow me to live my life without fear? Why couldn't I stop this curse?

Food and weight steered me. Every morning I woke up to another day I would attempt disciplined eating. Every hour was spent waiting to eat and then trying not to. Every place I went demanded a thought as to what foods would face me. Every plan I made included a goal to lose weight beforehand.

There was no such thing as "one." One cookie was not possible, therefore cookies were not allowed. Allowing myself chips, crackers, or anything with fat, salt, or sugar was asking for trouble. Salads, fruits, vegetables, and other foods that were not threatening would be all right, so I ate them in very large quantities to try to get satisfied. Any day I managed to eat these foods was a successful day.

I weighed myself daily to watch my progress. If I lost a pound or two my mood was happy and energetic. If I wasn't losing weight my mood was depressed, making it even more difficult to eat in control. Then, of course, after a few days, I would break away from the routine, slip into some "bad" foods, and find myself in bouts of uncontrollable eating.

My mornings and early afternoons were fine, until around four P.M., when I would find myself in the kitchen bringing out the contents of my refrigerator. My kids would be playing at this time and I occupied myself with crunchy, salty foods or just sampling whatever I found. This was why I couldn't have dinner. By the time my husband came home, I had consumed far more than I should have. Most foods I cooked for my family were foods I wasn't allowed. So I picked at the food and watched everyone else eat the meal I longed to have. This was a typical day.

At least once a week and usually more often, I found myself in unexplained, unstoppable, frenzied, and ferocious binges. A binge for me would reach many thousands of calories in a short period of time. Sometimes I would eat so much food that I would feel full and sick, only to go back and eat more a few hours later. The only way I can describe the sensation is to say that it felt like a switch had been flicked. Once it was on, there was no way to turn it off.

The cereal box had to be empty; the cookies had to be finished. Salty to sweet, bread and butter, crunchy to soft, then back to sweet again. I explored my cabinets, refrigerator, and freezer, searching to satisfy every craving. Since I knew I could not have these foods again for a long time, I needed to leave no container unturned. I must not leave anything out. I needed to enjoy all that food now so I wouldn't need it again.

Weekends were always disasters. If we had plans, I needed to have my weight at a certain number and that was my goal for the week. I would typically eat very little in the preceding days in order to prepare. Sometimes, as the weekend approached I ate out of control, not knowing why. Since that would make my weight go up, it led me to not want to go ahead with my plans. As I said, Sundays were never okay. They were the fight I never won. How I wished for a six-day week.

Wherever we were, no matter what time of day, if my bingeing had started while we were out, there was one more hurdle that made me afraid to go home: the kitchen. Coming home late at night, my husband would head upstairs. I didn't want him to stop me now. I'd wait to hear the water run as he washed up before going to bed, then I'd move into automatic. The cabinets were opened, the foods were pulled out, and then they were returned to their places. Like a good-night kiss that ends a day, I would turn off the lights and head up.

Then I would get ready for bed. Sick and defeated, devastated beyond reprieve. I just didn't want to be me. I would wash my face and look in the mirror to see the most distasteful girl. I leaned on the counter, close to the glass, supporting my chin in my hands. I talked to my face in the mirror, chanting the words "I hate you." I would lie in my bed and imagine the food traveling to the various parts of my body, feeling so helpless to stop their route. It felt like a poison to my progress, slowly killing my potential. Morning would come, a new chance to succeed with yet another goal to pursue. Don't eat. Burn it off. In a few days it will be okay.

I had a wonderful life. I loved my husband and inhaled my children. I appreciated all that we had. I didn't long for a change and actually wished it would stay the same. I was not unhappy about my life; I was unhappy about my weight. And I deplored my problems with food.

In my mind there was no hope to ever live a life free of obsessions with food. I didn't know anyone else who had this. I knew there were people with eating disorders who got too thin, vomited, or ate to obesity, but I had never heard of the kind of obsessing that I did. No one except my husband really knew, and he didn't know what to make of it or how he could help. And with all he knew, he knew only half. I was at a fine weight if judged by the standards of others. I worked out a lot in order to counter what I had eaten, so I had a decent figure. The days following "bad" eating, I made sure to eat very little. This would average out my weight. During the days when the scale went up, I pulled away from my life. I hid behind my kids' activities, wore bigger clothes, and buried myself under my secret.

As an adult, my weight had vacillated over the years. When I got married I was very thin, not that I could see it. I remember wishing I was just a bit thinner, and then I could have felt perfect. With my first pregnancy I put on more than forty pounds, and never lost all the weight. Depending on my binges and diets, I was between ten and fifteen pounds heavier than my prepregnancy weight. Had I been a hundred pounds more it wouldn't have made a difference. To me, it was insurmountable.

I used to look at thin people and decided they were one of two types. Either they were selfish or they were lucky, but both left me out of the picture. I would never be lucky enough not to need food, so forget any hope of that. And I would never allow myself that kind of freedom to let myself do what they did, whatever it was that they did. So forget hope of that one, too.

My life with food felt like prison. I felt like an inmate serving a sentence for a crime he didn't commit, waiting for some kind of break. Not able to understand how this could have happened to him, he dreams of the day he'll be free. No matter how long he's there, or how futile it seems, he has some hope of a release. One day someone will come to his cell, bang on the bars, and tell him it's time to go home. I prayed that day would come.

They say that prisoners, once free, repeat their crimes, due to a fear of life on the outside. Prison, while awful, has an element of safety due to the lack of choice and responsibility. It's structured and dependable. Freedom, while exhilarating, can be frightening. It leaves the door open to trouble and bad decisions. Prison can feel protective. And so can food obsessions.

To someone with eating and weight obsessions, food feels like living in an unsafe neighborhood, always in fear of attacks. It's an unsafe world of your own obsessions. You can lock all the doors, close all the windows, but there's nothing more to do. If they want to get in they'll get in.

The concept of life on the outside means taking full responsibility. The ex-convict would have to live honestly, and he hasn't a clue how to do that. For an ex–food convict, what would life be like without the food or food concerns? Would it feel like there would be nothing to look forward to, boring and sort of empty? Would there be an absence of comfort? Or would a life without food be the solution to the one last problem? And which is worse, the fear of staying in the prison or the fear of getting out?

Now that I'm living on the "outside," I have some answers to those questions. Breaking out is hard. Very hard. But living inside is harder. Living inside is full of diets, magazines, books, scales, articles, mirrors, and sizes. It's waiting for food, avoiding food, trying to cut something out. Living inside is searching for the answers. Maybe more protein, more exercise, cut out the bread and starches. Drink all liquids, fast for three days, find the latest herbs. Eat small portions, eat one meal a day, and never eat after six o'clock. Drink more water, avoid all sugar, and don't mix food groups together. Get a two-hundred-dollar enema; you'll lose three pounds in one day. And let's not forget surgery and the latest remedies for fat. Staple it, stretch it, or suck it all out. Ask about a prescription; it's so much less invasive. Inside is endless. Inside never works long-term. Successes are pounded down. Inside, too much self-esteem comes from one place. That place is thin and it's never thin enough.

Living on the outside, however, gathers all of that misdirected energy and focus, and shoots it into life. It goes to us. To who we are, what we really feel, what we really want, and what we would choose if we gave ourselves that choice. To accepting, finally, that our problems with weight have less to do with food and more to do with our needs. Not our need for food. Not our need to be thinner. It has to do with emotion. It has to do with life. It has to do with pain and discomfort, and how hard we must work not to feel it.

An obsession of any kind looks and feels like boundless energy put toward a task. What an obsession really is, however, is an avoided feeling, an avoided truth, or the avoidance of something that hurts. Something we don't want to face. Something we think we can't handle. We don't even know what it is. Or maybe, in fact, we do. The obsession is strong and all consuming. Doesn't it have to be? To keep us totally distracted and safe from feelings that are simply tremendous.

Remember I said that dieting felt like an iron gate? It kept me safe from eating by keeping food on the other side. In fact, it was that very obsession that kept me safe from *feelings*. It kept me on the other side of emotions. I wasn't even aware of them since food was all I could see.

If pain is there, and we're not sure it is, why would we want to feel that? What purpose would it serve? Why not continue to go on diets and eventually find one that works? Who's to say that isn't the answer, especially when life feels just fine? Well, let me pose some questions to you that I know you ask yourself. Questions you ask about food. *Why do I always need more? Why isn't it ever enough? Why can other people eat less and be fine, but for me that just couldn't cut it?*

Can you translate that to your life? What would it feel like to hear yourself say that in your life you want more? That in some relationships you may want more? Would it feel selfish and ungrateful and sound like you're complaining? Do you feel that even if you admitted it, it would be futile anyway? Since you're not even sure what you would want more of, or who you would want more with?

If you can somehow open your mind a bit, I want you to envision a gate. Not the one that keeps food away; this is a different one. This one keeps you from your own potential and the energy that you have to get there. All the things you want out of life but you could never let yourself have. Just like all the food you want but could never let yourself eat. Once you move beyond the food and through all the avoidance, you find yourself in a place, kind of like never-never land. All the things that you never believed could ever happen to you. I won't lie. Some of them are just awful. And some of them are magical, beyond any dream you have dreamed. So if obsessions are that strong, and, boy, are they ever, imagine that strength redirected. Holy smokes. Imagine that strength redirected.

Once you live outside of food you will have joy born of many places. You will also have many fears in your life, but they'll have nothing to do with food. There will be times you feel terrible frustration, but it won't be because you gained weight. Other times you'll feel terribly proud, but it won't come from losing weight. All of these feelings of pride and remorse will move from the scale to you. Physically, you'll have no complaints. But emotionally . . . well, there you'll have some gripes!

That comes only because you have already made the emotional choices necessary to live true to who you are and what you feel inside. This needs to be repeated. Your best physical self comes *after* you see what hides behind food and weight.

If you're tired of prison food, prison uniforms, prison rules, and prison life, start to plan your escape. You can share it with a friend or a family member or keep it all to yourself. You can start today, but you need to be ready. It won't work if you're too comfortable where you are. Of course, you're in a hurry. You'll do whatever it takes, yeah, yeah, yeah, let's just cut to the chase. The skinny one. Make me thin, you say, and I'll do anything you ask.

My name is Nancy and I've lived the life you call home. I lived inside for so many years and I'm here now to help you get out. Today I eat those foods that I craved, I'm thin, and I live my life. My weight is low because extra food is no longer what makes me feel better. I had to find out what would. My weight doesn't fluctuate all that much, but my emotions could break any scale!

Like an ex-convict who finally got out, I think about the others still there. Knowing what those cells feel like, I just want to raid the prison. I want to run inside and grab everyone and be their parole officer. I want to teach them a way to live so they won't end up back in the slammer. I understand all the fears and know they can't see a way out. But I won't stop until they do. Freedom just feels too good.

My food obsessions were not a curse. It was not the one horrible problem in a perfect life. It was a quiet scream. Inside me was another me. Apart from my decisions, choices, words, routines, and daily life she was tapping. I just didn't hear her. She tapped and tapped and tapped until finally I heard her voice. Bagel Day . . . I finally took her call. A call from me to me. And now I'm calling you. I'm outside your cell, banging on those bars. I'm here to take you home.

Chapter 2

Why should you listen to me? I am not a psychologist, dietitian, nutritionist, or doctor. I haven't studied the behaviors of hundreds of subjects, nor have I studied rats. I *am* the rat. I ran the maze, I ate the pellets, and I know what it felt like to be there. Am I an authority? You bet I am. Anyone who spends more than thirty years doing something is an authority on that subject. Unlike those who study from behind the glass, gathering data and notes, I was the one in the cage. If you want documentation of the rat's behaviors, go read up on their findings. If you want to know how the rat got out, you'll have to ask the rat.

To start, I can make you some promises. I promise to be honest even when it embarrasses me. I know it's the only way you'll trust me and I can't help you without it. I will show you where I feel strong and where I tread carefully, as it relates to food and emotions. I'll tell you what feels "safe" to me now and how I figure that out. Feeling safe with food comes from making safe choices in life. I'll go through it all, step by step, as though you're learning a choreographed dance. You will learn to separate the food in your life from feelings, responses, and choices.

I promise this will be, bar none, the hardest work you've ever done. You will get very tired and frustrated. You'll want to give up and I won't let you. You will feel hopeless and I will keep on giving you hope. You will insist on talking about the food and I'll insist that mostly we don't. You will want the quick fixes and I'll offer some to calm you. But if you try to use those fixes alone, and I refer here to food tricks and diets, I'll tell you right now it won't work. That's a promise, too.

You'll need to look at your goals. If you're anything like I was at the beginning, your goal is to lose weight and keep it off. If I told you we would not be dealing with weight loss right away, you'd last about as long as a bowl of chips on Sunday. I understand you because I understand me. So rest assured that as we begin to focus on what feelings sit behind food, we will also talk about food. How to eat and lose weight. That is literally what you'll have to do since you cannot lose weight by not eating.

You'll notice I said *goals* and not *goal*. Losing weight is one goal. If it's the only worthy goal you see, it's possible you'll still succeed. But, like with anything else, when you put all your efforts in one place, the pressure is overwhelming. And it may not ever be good enough since it leaves you with no other purpose. If you succeed in your goal to lose weight, what would you do with your life for a fresh challenge? I can hear the ad right now: "Looking for easy and convenient goals, open twenty-four/seven? Weight Loss. You don't even have to leave home."

One pound gained makes you feel like a failure; one pound lost and you're on top of the world. Imagine life beyond that one pound. Unimaginable, I know. The more goals you have outside of your weight, the less that pound will matter. The more needs you fill in other places, the less need you'll have for food. The hand-me-down will be weight loss.

You will be learning to eat, instead of what you've been trying unsuccessfully to do, which is to not eat. You cannot lose weight without eating. Depriving yourself is like sending an invitation to a binge by FedEx. You will learn how to eat, you will learn how to stop, and you'll learn why it's been such a problem. In the end, you're going to walk into any situation and find you have choices. Choices of what you want to eat, and what you want to do.

My last promise is that you can beat this. I know you don't believe that. I didn't believe it either. But here I am today, and I came from the same place as you. It is a hopeless, endless, and impossible place where food speaks louder than words. We need to listen to those feelings inside and not let the food drown them out.

Hunger will seem more like background noise when it comes from a healthy place. You'll need to quiet down other things though, like feelings that bang and clammer. One day you will look back and say, "Man, no wonder I used food to suppress. My feelings hurt like hell!"

How will you get to those feelings? I will teach you to use your eating nightmares as the best informer you have. You'll be going on a treasure hunt and the food will serve as your clue. You may choose to work with a therapist to help you even further. You may find support from books, lectures, seminars, or workshops. This will be your own work in progress and you'll find what feels right to you.

At times you'll take steps forward and feel very successful. You'll think you finally licked it; no more food problems here! Then you'll have a setback and feel like you're getting nowhere. That is true of emotions, too. Sometimes you think you are over anger and then it gets triggered again. Responses can change from day to day, and you're going to start feeling that more.

You and I are connected by these responses we have in common. I used to have them with food just as you do today. Here's my good news. I don't have those obsessions with food anymore and I don't have problems with weight. Here's the bad news. The emotions are just as horrendous. We food-obsessed folk are emotional people. We feel things very deeply. That emotional depth and intensity, *not food,* can feel like our unlucky curse. It is also our finest feature. You are not where you are because you are weak. You are not weak at all. To the contrary, my friend, you have an unstoppable strength, and when you live past the food you will need it.

Anytime you doubt your inner strength, your ability to focus, and your boundless energy to succeed, just recall all the "failures" in diets. Did you give up? No. You found another one, and if that didn't work you found more and more. You are relentless in your desire and motivation to succeed. Look at just the time factor. Don't you see the minutes, the hours, and the amount of thoughts in your head?

The research you do in the form of diets. The experts whose advice you seek and the articles you read up on. The planning and follow-through. The conversations you have with people to share ideas on the subject. The commitment and dedication you show toward something you really want. How frustrating this has been. All of this work and energy without the reward of completion.

When you direct that energy to life and love, and not to diet and weight, you'll be extremely successful in both of these places due to your infinite perseverance. Your problems will be in real-life issues, not imagined food ones. Your problems will be in relationships that you face honestly without fear. Or you face honestly *with* fear. Just so long as you face them. Your success will come from goals that excite you, not scales that get old and tired. Maintaining your weight isn't nearly as hard when you make it the second goal. Or third. The mistake was in putting it first.

When you face issues upfront, you gain. Not weight, but choices. When you confront the feelings that hurt and frighten, you learn what willpower is. Willpower is not about sticking to diets, it's about sticking to the truth. It's about being strong enough to say "This is who I am," not "This is what I weigh." When you begin to live close to the person who lives inside you, food loses its control over you. People lose control over you, too.

You have been misrepresented to yourself. You have talked yourself into believing that you can't stop eating because you aren't strong enough to say no. In fact, you'll discover you have not learned to say no, but it has nothing to do with eating.

There are things going on in your life, apart from food, that you want to say no to. There are people, events, situations, and choices being made that are not what you want. Once you learn to say "No, this is not what I choose," and make another choice instead, you will be able to make choices with food that feel just as strong and knowing.

There is one place where *no* has no value, and that is in the life situations where there is no choice, and you have no control. It is what it is. Saying no would put you in a nonaccepting state, and that is an impossible place to live. Here you must say yes. Yes, it's happened; yes, it is; and yes, I need to accept it. Once you say yes in acceptance, you will also say yes to food. Yes, I can eat this and

I won't lose control. Yes, I can eat in a controlled manner even though there are things in my life I cannot control. And yes, saying yes feels terrifying at times.

Controlling your food is not the answer to feeling in control. The answer is knowing which parts of your life, outside of food, you can control and which parts of your life, outside of food, you can't. And finding your peace in both. *Yes* is wonderful in your life. Not "Yes, I am allowed to eat this," but "Yes, I'm allowed to feel this; yes, I'm allowed to do this; yes, I'm allowed to make this choice because this is what's right for me."

There's someone inside you who needs to come out. This person is very strong, very dynamic, and capable in extraordinary measure. Part of you has been sitting on the bench, waiting in your own "time out." There's a restlessness, a stirring, and a growling in your stomach. It's not the hunger you thought it to be; that growl is a beast of potential. You have a *voice* that longs to be heard; it's time to learn how to listen.

Chapter 3

Whenever I used to pick up a self-help book about losing weight, I'd skim the table of contents to get past the mumbo jumbo. I would jump ahead to the chapters that had the eating and losing-weight parts. So I could lose the weight *now*. What if I told you that the losing-weight parts are in the chapters that aren't about food? Would you believe me and read those other parts first? Or would you go to the food chapters right away so you can lose weight *now*. Yeah, that's what I thought. I know you like a book!

You may think I'm being controlling or manipulative by not heading the chapters with titles. Here's another promise. I will always protect you here. Because of my understanding of you, due to my understanding of me, I can lead you through these pages in the order I believe you should read them. Remember, you came to me for help. My job is to steer you differently than you would steer yourself.

I know you're not long on patience right now and you need to start getting answers. I know you've exhausted every vehicle. If something doesn't work right away, you think it won't work at all. So here's what I'm going to tell you. Stay with me. If you feel my approach doesn't work fast enough, just wait it out a bit.

Remember the restaurant that had too long of a wait so you left it to find someplace else? And once you got there, they had a long wait, too? So you went to a third place with an even longer line? In your impatience and refusal to wait, it ended up taking you longer than if you had simply not left the first place. Stay here. And chew on this while you wait:

I am handing you tools to start with now, and you'll keep learning new ways to use them. If they don't make sense or seem comfortable yet, they will at a later point. You may find that you see results in your eating habits right away. If you don't see results, not to worry. It's been only a few pages and we hardly know each other.

Go to the store and buy yourself at least two notebooks. In the first book, put the day and date on the top of the first page. This is your food diary. You need to take a look at what you're eating and what's going on around you. You've tried this before? Try it again with me. You're in a different place now, no matter where that place is. It may end up feeling quite different.

Write down every single piece of food that goes into your mouth. You'll need to write down where you are, what you're doing, and who you're with or if you're alone. Also, write down the time of day the food is eaten. You don't need to change what you're doing or try to eat less. Just keep track of it. Later, when we're looking at eating patterns, you'll need to monitor where you seem to eat more and where food seems less of a problem.

Begin to notice hunger. Try to distinguish between what we've often heard as stomach hunger and mouth hunger. Stomach hunger refers to real hunger. Mouth hunger does not. Be conscious of eating when you notice that feeling in your stomach. If you don't know what that feeling is, go without eating until you feel it. If you can't go without eating until you feel it, that's okay, too. It's just another thing to notice. This is all about discovering the way your food world works and what your patterns are.

Although you're not yet aware of it, every bit of eating you're doing is being triggered by something else. If it's not hunger (and most of us aren't really sure what that is anymore) it's absolutely something happening in that moment. Don't be fooled by moments where it seems like nothing is happening. Emotionally something is. You will learn to be an expert at figuring that out, but right now you're just taking notes. The sooner you get yourself doing this, the closer you will be to freedom.

This one's a tool for life. Begin to imagine your food as something that needs to be organized. For example, if you have an office, picture your food as folders and materials on a desk. Imagine you've come back after being gone a few days and your work has piled up. Everything is all over the place and you feel too overwhelmed to get started. When eating is all over the place, it's impossible to feel in control. Picking at food mindlessly is the desk with folders all scattered.

Now imagine that desk neatly organized with piles distributed in order of importance so you can prioritize what you need to tend to first. When eating is structured, neat, and not chaotic, you feel more in control. Liken this to any aspect of your life. Organized toy rooms are easier to play in; cars feel better when they're clean. Purses, closets, offices, and homes are easier to deal with when organized and uncluttered with junk. This means eating meals on a plate just like a human being. Just because you see something edible doesn't mean you stick it in your mouth. Keep the structure of meals and snacks. Like folders opened and closed as you need them, and then put away when you're finished.

Your food can be whatever you want it to be. It isn't so much about what you're eating but how you are eating it. More about that later. For now, just be aware of structure. Later, we'll be going through your life and finding ways to put things in order; this includes food, emotions, personal affects, and routines. Begin to notice the calming effects of organization in all the facets of your day.

This is not a tool. This is a simple fact and one you need to know. You'll hear it more as we go along because this one is that important. Deprivation leads to overeating. The more you tell yourself you can't have it, the more you'll want and need it. Each time you stay away from the foods you crave, you set yourself up to eat more. Deprivation also leads to bingeing. I know you and you will still deprive yourself because you don't know another way. That's okay for now. But say it every day. Every time you deprive a craving I want you to recite it again. *Deprivation leads to overeating.* Whatever you refuse to give yourself now, you'll end up paying for later. In the form of eating more. Let's talk about this for a minute.

Recall every single thing in your life you couldn't have but wanted so badly. What was that wanting like? Once you got it, if you did, was it all you thought it would be? Did you tire of it quickly and move on to something new that you couldn't have? Try to remember the things you wanted and finally got. The great-looking guy or girl, the car, the outfit, money, success, or home.

Was the guy or girl that great? Did success solve all your problems? Of course not. But you liked the date, enjoyed the money, and the home is just wonderful. I know, you're wondering what's the point.

The point is that when you let yourself have that treat, it takes the energy and focus out of wanting it so badly. Your fear, as was mine, is that eating a doughnut will make you fat. Your fear is that you'll need more than one. The reality is that one doughnut does not make you fat. Three doughnuts do not make you fat. The deprivation combined with the fear cause you to obsess. That longing causes you to give in to cravings in a "gotta have it now" kind of way. Since you believe that on a normal basis you can't have doughnuts. Not if you want to be thin. Here's the news flash: You *can* have it on a normal basis. Heard that before somewhere? Goody. You just heard it again!

Time for the second notebook. While the first notebook records all of your food and food situations, this one will record the dialogue inside your head. If you think there is no dialogue in your head, then writing will prove you wrong. What you don't know is what's hurting you. Your notebook will connect you to what's going on inside. Just as 3-D movies cannot be seen without wearing those funny glasses, putting a pen to paper, or hands to the keyboard, allows dimension. I don't know what makes those glasses work, and I don't know why writing brings different perspectives. I know only that it draws a new picture every single time.

You don't have to be a writer, you just need to write. You don't need to have something to write about. Sit down where it's quiet or sit where there's noise and just write. If you don't know what to write, then write about not knowing what to write. Just like the

3-D movie, things pop out at you and you feel like reaching toward them. This book, not the one you're reading but the one you'll write, is going to become one of the most important things in your life. It is going to connect you to yourself, and that's who we're looking for.

Chapter 4

I want to talk about the Bagel Day. With any given situation, particularly those that cause us pain, there is a point we can reach when we break. It may be a relationship, a job, a friendship, a transition, an injury to our body or soul; but we know we cannot go on. Not that way. And that is the moment we surrender.

The next moment presents a choice. We either get back up and continue doing what we've been doing, or we make a decision to move on. Staying the course may feel different for a while because we find a way to accept and live with the pain. It's not bad all the time, but when it's bad, oh, it's bad. I once caught my face in the mirror in the middle of acceptance like that. Whoa. I was one scaaaary-lookin' animal.

Moving on, on the other hand, requires a change. Not a change of address necessarily, not another partner or job, although these changes may occur; sometimes moving on simply means making a choice to live differently inside of the same situation. That means that the circumstances stay the same but we become changed within them. We cannot change who we are, but we can change how we react and respond. We decide to take control.

Control is a tough one. There is so much in life, as we're constantly reminded, that we have no say in, no knowledge of, no choice in, and no chance to stop. However, there are things we do have control over. Many of the small details of a day are in our control. What we wear, who we speak to, where we shop, where we drive to, what time we go to bed, what music we play, and how we vote in elections.

And then, of course, there are the things we know, intellectually, we should be able to control, yet we feel powerless. At times we cannot control our anger. Can't stop feeling so sad. Can't control our excitement or can't stay away from a man. That woman makes us crazy, that child makes us scream. We cannot control our temper, and our anxiety takes on a life of its own. Our depression just comes when it wants to and the weather affects our moods. Oh, and lest I forget, we cannot control our food.

What led me to pick up that phone on that very day, which was only a replica of so many days just like it, was that it was the moment I broke. I had reached my limit. I could not live that way any longer. The call on that day was to my doctor. "I think I have an eating disorder," I said. "I'm sure you do, everyone does," he said lightly, and he told me who to call. Our local hospital had a clinic, so I looked up the number and called. I set up an appointment for a consultation and instantly felt some hope.

This was a bold move on my part. I wasn't buying into another magazine with another solution. I wasn't going up to a thin friend or stranger and asking her what she ate. And I wasn't having another binge followed by days of dieting. This was a reach outside my cell. It was an arm through the bars and a call to the world outside. I knew this one move would require a leak of my private shame in some public situation. To sit in a waiting room would require an admission of imperfection, and I could appear unbalanced. I made sure to schedule the appointment in a few days' time; I needed to lose a few pounds and look good!

I sat in the waiting room with a couple of other people. I tried to look like I didn't belong. I filled out forms that told me I was most definitely in the wrong place. They asked if I ever thought about harming myself, had severe depression, had cutting episodes, or was hospitalized. No, no, no, my pencil proudly followed the column. I knew they would probably send me home; this was no place for someone with a little lack of self-control. I didn't have any problems like these poor people. I just needed some minor tweaking, thank goodness.

A woman about my age came and called my name. She introduced herself as Melinda. She looked like a Melinda. She had a fun, easy look about her. She was blond, very thin, with a casual, comfortable style. I liked her. I wondered if she had an eating disorder and admitted it, or if she had an eating disorder and denied it, but I knew she had to have one. She was thin. I wanted to ask her what she ate but I refrained. She asked me to tell her why I was there, a little about myself, my life, and my history with food behaviors. I told her everything. She was so easy for me to talk to. But my mind kept visiting another thought as well: what it would feel like to sit in a chair with her flat stomach and thin, muscular legs.

When we finished, she told me she was an eating-disorders therapist herself but her schedule was completely full. I told her I wanted someone like her, someone I would feel just as comfortable with. She explained that she would look at the availability of the other therapists who she thought would be a good match for me, and would call me in a few days with a name. Pretty painless. I waited for her call.

As promised, Melinda got back to me with a name. I called to set up the appointment. Dressed like the happy, well-adjusted girl I was, I returned to the same waiting room. As I waited, watching people go in and out, I saw a well-dressed woman walk out of an office with another person who I presumed to be her patient. She asked if I had been taken care of. I told her I was waiting to see Jenny. She told me to wait and that she should be coming out soon. She went back in her office and closed the door.

Just a couple of minutes later, she opened the door, walked back out, walked over to me, and held out her hand. "I'm Jenny," she said. Excuse me? What exactly was that? I quietly and uncomfortably remarked, "Oh, I didn't know that was you." She didn't respond to that but led me back to her office. We sat down as she began looking over my forms. I didn't know quite what to do. I was so put off and uneasy with this woman. I found that introduction to be anything but comfortable, normal, or kind. I gathered my courage and asked why she didn't identify herself when I told her who I was waiting for.

She moved around in her chair with her stupid-looking shoes and said, "Oh, I don't know, I suppose I should have said who I was."

There was not much that was going to turn this around for me. I had a very uneasy feeling, but, even more than that, I simply didn't like her. I told her my story anyway. I told her about my fabulous husband, my beautiful kids, and my very fortunate life. I told her a little history and let her know that in my mind, I just had this problem with food that I would like to get taken care of. She talked with me a bit and then gave me one tidbit to take with me until our next appointment. One sentence to start me off on the direct, non-stop trip to my cure. "Deprivation leads to bingeing," she said. "Thank you" is what I said to her face. "See you soon, *not,*" was what I said to myself. I went home to call Melinda.

I told Melinda the whole story. She didn't question my feelings, but she told me Jenny was a very good therapist and I might want to try one more time. I thought about her stiff shoes, the way she squirmed in her chair, and the way I felt in that office. I told Melinda I just wanted to feel comfortable, the way I felt with her. "Okay," she said, and followed it with what came as a complete surprise: "I'll just find a way to squeeze you into my schedule." I was overjoyed and thankful.

My happiness at her response was short-lived, however, when I found out there was a hitch. Melinda told me I had to call Jenny and explain why I wanted to switch. "OH, PLEASE DON'T MAKE ME DO THAT. Can't you call her instead?" Melinda explained it would be a healthy part of the process for me to confront my feelings and put closure on the situation. Closure, to me, was something I did with Ziplocs. I had no desire to have it with Jenny. It wasn't my fault I didn't like her, and Melinda was right there in the office. It would be easy enough for her to tell her. Melinda insisted I make the call, and she was not backing down. This felt like hell week; I got into the house of my choice, and this was part of my hazing.

Jenny picked up the phone. I told her who it was. I described my reaction to what had happened and the discomfort I still had because of it. I told her I had decided not to continue my therapy with her and would instead be seeing Melinda. She was very accepting of what I said and much more genuine in her manner than she had been when we met. I could hear that she was regretful that it had started in such a way. She suggested that perhaps we try to meet again, and that it's not unusual for the first session to feel awkward and uncomfortable. She apologized for how it had been handled.

I felt for her. I knew she was sorry and I believed her to be sincere. I felt myself being pulled back into seeing her, not because I wanted to but because I would feel too guilty not to. And then I remembered Melinda. I recalled the instant comfort and ease. I knew this was my lifeline and I couldn't give it up to spare Jenny's feelings. I told her how much I appreciated everything she had said. I said I was also sorry we had started off this way, but I really believed this was the best decision for me at the time. I thanked her; we wished each other well and ended the conversation.

Melinda was right. That was a call I needed to make. Ironically, as I look back it illustrates so perfectly what I went on to learn about the importance of choice and control. That one event held all of these lessons: Look into a situation; assess how you feel; evaluate your choices and make a decision; if that decision leads you to more choices, evaluate again; don't make decisions based on guilt or pressure; don't be talked into doing something that isn't right for you.

Making that phone call was a huge step in taking responsibility for my feelings and decisions. It was instrumental in teaching me to deal with circumstances that are uncomfortable but unavoidable in life. It taught me about standing up for myself and giving my choice a voice. I felt powerful in that call. I had felt slighted somehow by this woman. She had treated me like a patient with no person underneath, and I didn't like how it felt.

It wasn't about forgiveness. This was more about trust and comfort. My decision had to come from my feelings, without regard for hers. I was simply making a choice. That choice, I believe, was one of the more critical ones of my life. I followed my gut, went with my instinct, and trusted my knowledge of me. Hell week was over; I was officially in. Alpha O-may-i Eat-a-pie.

How does this tie into food? I'll tell you exactly how. Making that phone call made me anxious, nervous, and extremely uncomfortable, but it was in honest keeping with what I wanted. Had I made the call, followed Jenny's suggestion, and met with her again,

I can guarantee you that after the call or before our next appointment I would have had a binge.

When you go against what you feel, when you fight the nature of who you are, it causes you to scream. If the scream doesn't come from your voice or your actions, it comes out in the way you eat. The bigger the betrayal to yourself, the bigger the out-of-control food behavior. Jenny was right. Deprivation leads to bingeing. But it's not only in food. Deprivation of voice can be worse, when it sits inside unheard.

When I look back at my beginning, a beginning that would have been unnoteworthy had I not been instructed to make that call, I'm struck by the two very important messages I received. Jenny's was a food truth; her message that deprivation leads to bingeing was critical in working out my food issues. Melinda's was life-related, and the key to emotional survival. If you had asked me at that time which advice I was more focused on, I would have told you it was the one about food. If you ask me today what solved the mysteries of my problems with food, there's simply no doubt in my mind. The clues were not hidden in food. They were deep inside my life.

Chapter 5

When I was about ten years old, every Monday night I used to turn on *The Doris Day Show*. She was bright, happy, cheery, and funny. She was blond and full of life. She was pretty but not the intimidating kind. You just had to love her. I wanted to be like her. Between Doris Day and Goldie Hawn, I found who I wanted to be.

That's who walked into Jenny's office and that's who began sessions with Melinda. Blond, sunny, happy, and fizzy; yep, that was me, Doris Day. With a double splash of Goldie. Their style never pushes people away. They allure with glittering light. You can't help but want to be near them.

Melinda asked questions about my past, my family, my husband, Scott, and my life. This was a waste of precious time and dollars. I was thinking, Let's get to the food; that's why I'm here, isn't it? I'm happy with my life, and besides that I've had therapy in the past when I've needed it. Therapy is not what I need right now. I need to talk about my eating.

I wonder if I was typical of what walks through those doors. Certainly from the forms I filled out I imagine that most of the people are not coming in singing. Ironically, those are the ones who are better off; at least they know they have problems. I, on the other hand, was Doris/Goldie. I had a lot further to go.

Melinda instructed me to monitor my food. That meant write it down. This, she explained, would give her an idea of what, when, and how I was eating. She told me not to try to alter what I was doing; this was simply a record. I wrote down the days that represented what, at the time, were considered "normal" days for me. I also recorded the days of overeating and binges, as they occurred. Recovering from an episode of that kind of eating required heavy-duty dieting for days; I recorded that, too. I wrote down every piece of food that went into my mouth.

The pages I brought to Melinda were usually quite long. I was eating so many different foods in small bites, picks, samples, and tastes that the paper looked like a shopping list for a day camp. I never ate breakfast. Anytime I started eating in the morning it set me up to eat all day, and badly at that. No food allowed before noon. The unfortunate part of this was that my very favorite foods were breakfast foods. I loved cereal, breads, pancakes, waffles, eggs, and French toast. It would have been far too risky to have any of those foods at any time, so I simply stayed away from them.

Lunches were large and basically the same every day. I ate salads of enormous quantity. You may not understand what I mean by *enormous*. My husband once opened the refrigerator and said, "Well, I see all the Nancy food. Is there any food for the rest of us?" Quantity was something I allowed as long as it was healthy and not fattening. It was an effort to satisfy myself since I couldn't eat any of the foods I really wanted. To look at the kitchen after my lunch was prepared, you would have thought I had just entertained the PTA. My lunch was an event.

Somewhere around four o'clock in the afternoon, I began picking and sampling an array of my allowed foods. I ate a lot of rice cakes because they were crunchy and low in fat. I would dip into frozen yogurt out of the carton and sample whatever I was making Scott for dinner. The kids ate earlier so I ate crusts and leftovers of their dinner. There was no plate of food, no meal per se. It was a three-hour period of eating a little bit of everything.

When Scott came home around seven o'clock, I had a beautiful dinner all ready. We would sit and eat dinner together. I sat, he ate. There was one fork, one knife, and one glass of water. I never ate dinner with him. I just watched. I envied each bite he took.

Sometimes I would chew on the chicken bones he had cut most of the meat from, or eat the skin of his potato. I'd even eat the skin from his fish. Thank goodness we had no dog; we would have had to compete. I knew that with all the food I had eaten before, I couldn't afford to eat more.

This was not something he questioned. He knew about my eating on Sundays since I would complain it was a "five-pound day." If I wasn't eating dinner with him, he knew I had probably overeaten that day. It wasn't that I kept it from him. As a matter of fact, he could tell when I had terrible eating days just by the look on my face. "Oh, you binged, didn't you?" As if it were just a bad part of my day, he felt sad for me and then moved on.

Sometimes I would go through the days feeling fine about my eating. Once in a while, though, I was hit. Like riding a bike with the direction of traffic, you can't see what's coming from behind; my eating was much like that. I didn't get a warning. There was no sign I was in danger. By the time I sensed that approaching car, it was too late to get away. I was in the midst of a binge, not knowing how I could stop it. There was only one way to fix it. Exercise and diet like crazy.

Weekends were consistent and predictable. It was never a question of not eating. The question was simply how much. Friday nights were a fight not to eat snacky foods if we sat around to watch TV or a rented movie. Saturdays were usually okay during the day because I was motivated to keep my weight down for our plans that evening. Typically we had a baby-sitter and met friends to go out for dinner. This was quite involved.

Sometimes I found myself eating out of control during the day, which horrified me. I knew that would make it impossible to find something to wear that evening. I would feel too fat to go. If I hadn't been eating much during the day, I found myself too hungry to wait. Since I didn't allow myself dinner-type foods anyway, thinking they would make me gain weight, I would often have something to eat before we left.

Restaurants rarely served anything I could feel safe eating. Some of them had salads and I would order them without dressing. Sometimes I would get a vegetable plate if I was lucky enough to be somewhere that served them. I dreaded going since it meant sitting and watching everyone else eat. When we came home later, and this was inevitable, I went straight to the kitchen and headed right for the food.

Sundays were bad from the start. I would make breakfast for Scott. I would pick off his plate. While he read the paper, I would begin eating other things, too. Or, we'd take the kids out for a late-morning brunch. I'd order a fruit plate in order to try to eat lightly. I'd end up eating the grilled-cheese crusts, tastes of omelets, pancakes, and fries from everyone else's plate. Once we got home, since the switch had been flicked, I continued to eat in my kitchen. And since just about every weekend we went to Scott's family's for dinner, the nightmare had just begun. Sundays felt like driving a car that didn't have any brakes. I knew I was going to crash.

Melinda and I began to study the patterns, focusing on those binges. What was happening? "Nothing," I would insist. "You don't understand my sisters-in-laws' houses on Sundays. Nothing is going on, but the very second you walk in, the food is everywhere." Melinda would tell me, "Nancy, it's not about the food. There is something else going on." "You don't see it," I would tell her. "They have Doritos and this layered taco dip, spinach dip, shrimp, herring, and peanuts with raisins, barbecued chicken, skirt steaks, hamburgers, chocolate chip cookies, coffee cake, brownies, and ice cream cake. There's licorice bites all over the place and a pantry stocked with back-ups. You're wrong," I'd say. "It *is* about the food." I knew this because every time we got in the car to go, the anxiety would begin. I knew that the second I walked through the door I would make my way to the food. There was no way to stop it and I knew that. Of course it was the food.

Insisting that we needed to look deeper into those Sundays, Melinda questioned me about Scott's family. No dark secrets there. There was one word I would use to describe coming into his family. Blessed. I felt extremely fortunate to be a part of such a wonderful group of people. They were fun, warm, and generous beyond any generosity I had ever known. They were kind, considerate, and always planners of fun. They embraced my presence and made me feel loved and accepted. I could not have asked for more. This is why I told Melinda I knew the problem was food. What else could it be?

Chapter 6

Tuesdays. My home got cleaned once a week. Not the home I lived in, but the home inside my head. If I had to describe my sessions with Melinda, it felt like walking through a big old house with lots of rooms. Each room was off a hall and all the doors were shut. Each room represented some section of my life, a period of time, a relationship, or a response to a part of my day.

Once a week, on those Tuesdays, we'd open a door and start to work on that room. It required taking a good, hard look at everything in that space, identifying what it meant to me, and getting familiar with the feelings it evoked. Every room we visited I had hoped would be the one. The one that I could look in and say, "Oh-ho, that was the problem!" And then the food would be gone.

I, of course, wanted to surface-clean. My goal was to get the room done fast to see if this was the one causing my eating. I wanted to take the feather-duster approach and sweep it across the room. Melinda wanted to detail-clean, just like my grandmother would have. Melinda was removing cushions from couches, seeing what was underneath them. Melinda wanted to clean the grout, and get down to the baseboards. I was thinking, *Has this skinny bitch got any clue that I need this weight off by Friday?* This week we've got a party to go to and I need to wear that black skirt. I am not interested in detail-cleaning, but how 'bout a cleaning crew! This was taking way too long and my patience was beginning to wear.

Those first few months, I brought my journal in with me. I had marked down all my food. My weight each day headed a page, followed by every bite that went into my mouth. Our discussions could be anything that was on my mind. Situations would arise in my life, but I was afraid that if I spent too much time on them, I wouldn't lose any weight. I was in a nervous state about my eating. I wasn't seeing any changes or progress as a result of my therapy. This was not the kind of fix I had initially hoped for. I started to lose trust in Melinda.

I continued with the therapy, but I expressed my feelings of hopelessness and my loss of confidence in what we were doing. I repeatedly asked Melinda if people really got over this. Were there people as deeply entrenched as I who survived it? She assured me there were. But there were also those who could not let it go. She made one thing very clear to me. There were reasons why I needed the food. Reasons why I needed the obsessions and the cycles. She pointed to the fact that this was a self-created pattern. One day Melinda asked me point-blank, "What would it be like without the food? Tell me, Nancy, what would your life be like without the food?" It didn't take me long to answer. "Boring."

Her question forced me to see what the food did for me. It gave me a project, something to focus on, worry about, and engage myself in. After time, I began to understand the cycle. Like framing a house just to knock it down and then having to build it again. The goal could never be met, so I never needed a new one. Dieting and deprivation, a way to lose weight. Overeating and bingeing, a way to gain it back. Diet, binge, diet, binge, diet, binge. If that goal was ever met, what would my new challenge be? What else would I do?

The diets I tried were unlivable long-term, which led to the overeating. For example, once I tried a protein diet. It was late morning and I craved an apple. I couldn't have an apple because fruits were a no-no if I was to do this right. I had some meat in the fridge, and figured I would eat that. I kept eating slice after slice; this, after all, was legal. I ended up gaining two pounds that day, when all I wanted was a friggin' apple!

Depriving myself of anything led me to eat even more. But that was the surface-cleaning answer. I had to move the couch, pick up the rug, and see what lay beneath. It was there and had been for a while. An absolute housekeeping disaster. A task too hard to take on. The food was the furniture hiding the dirt that was too big a job to face. You'll never believe what I found: I was unhappy in my life. Who would have ever thunk it?

It was the last thing I expected to find. I thought I loved my life. I was so fortunate in all that I had and I don't even mean materially. Money was something we had very little of in the first years of our marriage. We struggled quite a bit, but never argued about it at all. And much later, when more money began coming in, it didn't change anything about us. It just changed the way we could live. Either way, money or not, we loved the way we lived life.

But our happy life was covering up some extremely unhappy feelings. Melinda knew it was not the food, and now I could see it, too. But where was all this therapy stuff getting me? Before I was happy in my life but couldn't stop eating. Now I was unhappy in my life and still couldn't stop eating. And I was supposed to pay her for this? Fortunately, there was something else I didn't know. I still had a long way to go.

I began to get better about identifying where the eating was coming from. By looking at the journals I kept, I could pretty much figure out the source. The first time it happened was when Melinda questioned me about some Saturday night plans we had coming up. I was focused on being thinner for that evening. She asked who the plans were with and what our relationship was to these people. I talked about my discomfort with some of them. And then she asked me a question. "Nancy, do you even like these people?" I stopped and thought for a second. I was so shocked to hear my answer. "No, I guess I really don't like these people." Whoa.

Annie Sullivan spelled W-A-T-E-R in Helen Keller's hands as the water poured from the pump. Annie had been signing in her hands for months. Finally one day, the wires connected and Helen burst with understanding. She couldn't run fast enough from object to object with Annie's hand to spell it for her. Helen's world had opened up. Like Helen, connecting words to objects, I began to connect eating to life. In Melinda's hands, I was learning to read my emotions. Finally my world would open.

Chapter 7

I went back down the hall. The one inside my head. I wanted to go through all of those rooms, now that I knew how to clean them. I had direction. I was learning to make some choices. But the rooms were full and cluttered, and not just with objects of life. Those rooms were full with people.

I opened the door, looked inside, and there she was. My mom. So much to go through here, and at the time I wasn't sure it was worth it. Not because I didn't love her; I very much love my mom. But there was so much old stuff and it seemed futile to try to clean it. I couldn't change our past, couldn't change who she was, and couldn't change how I felt. But I knew one thing for sure. There wasn't a day I spent at my mom's house that I didn't head straight for her pantry, search the fridge, and stuff myself with food. That's how I knew to open this door; I could smell the food inside.

Melinda and I talked a lot about my childhood and my relationship with my mom, as a teenager and, currently, as an adult. We talked about my disappointment, my anger, my hurt, and my blame. I blamed my mom for not being there the way she should have. I blamed my mom for events that took place in our lives. I blamed her for the way she dealt with everyone in my family. And finally, the deepest blame of all, I believed she didn't love me enough. My mom just didn't love me the way I needed to be loved.

I was aware when I hugged my mom that something stood between us. I felt as though I were coated in something that sealed me from feeling it. I felt horrible about that since I knew my mom felt the hugs that she gave me. I wanted to feel them, too. I just didn't know how to get past this.

Melinda and I dissected my relationship with my mom. I wasn't unfamiliar with the disappointments of my past. What I didn't know was how deeply devastating the feelings still were and how much I had suppressed them. There was good reason to put them away. I wanted to have a close relationship with my mom. I wanted to spend time with her. To admit and face those painful feelings could have disengaged us. It was safer to see only good.

With Melinda, these emotions were right there at the front door. Day-to-day conversations and events with my mom were becoming more difficult now. I had tapped into the resentment. It was like digging deep in the sand with a shovel and suddenly hitting something hard. These feelings had been there a very long time, buried beneath time and events. Now that I had found that rock, I couldn't bury it again.

The rock was our history, deep inside our relationship, and that's why the food was so overwhelming. It's why I needed to eat the minute I walked inside her house. The food was a destination to keep me away from those feelings.

Whatever interactions my mom and I had were harshly judged by me now, no matter how insignificant. I judged her generosity, or what I considered to be a lack thereof. I judged if she was being thoughtful. I judged personal decisions in her life having nothing to do with me. I was running a tab on everything she did in the past on up to the present. I wanted to be a good daughter, but I carried the bag with those feelings. The weight of that bag made it very hard to act like I carried nothing.

While I was seeing Melinda, I never approached my mom with any of the feelings brought out in my therapy. I believed it was all in the past and that was where it should stay. But as long as we're on the subject, let me jump ahead to tell you why that changed. It wasn't until a couple of years after I stopped seeing Melinda that I finally confronted my mom.

It happened unexpectedly. She was visiting us at our house in the country and we had gone out for a walk. In the course of our conversation she made a comment that set me off. It was sort of an accusation that I was being ungenerous in my hospitality toward her and my stepfather Charles. She made it seem as though she were a victim, due to the fact that I was being unyielding. You'll need some background here.

Often during the summer, when friends and family come out to visit, we invite them to stay overnight. At that time, when my mom would come out to see us, she usually stayed just for the day. If she came out alone, I encouraged her to spend the night. If she came out with Charles, I didn't extend the same invitation. It's not that I had said no. But I believed she knew not to ask. She knew that my relationship with him was limited, to say the least.

I knew the reasons for my lack of hospitality were a direct result of the discomfort I had when I was with them. I couldn't let her think I was ungenerous because I am one of the more generous people I know. I made a decision in that very moment; she needed to know what I knew. She needed to know what I felt. I just couldn't hold it any longer, so I emptied that bag in her lap.

I told her what it had felt like as a child to live with a man I barely knew. I told her I never understood why there had been no efforts made to ease us into the new family we had become. Then I told her how it affected me in relationships as an adult, in my relationship with my husband, and even with intimacy. I let her know I had kept it from her because I hadn't wanted to hurt her. I didn't want to blame her. But now she was blaming me. And that I just couldn't take. I wasn't to blame for the feelings I had in response to things she was part of.

If I ever seemed ungenerous, that wasn't it at all. It was just that I was uncomfortable and didn't know how to get past it. Decisions I made with regard to her were influenced by many past issues. Decisions I made in regard to Charles were influenced by that discomfort. All of the family occasions, dinners, and gatherings were fine and I had adjusted to them. Formerly, that adjustment meant devouring Wheat Thins and candy, and stuffing myself at those meals.

As an adult, and with the help of Melinda, I had learned to be there with the feelings and stay there without the crackers. Inviting

Charles to sleep in my house was where I drew the line. It would have felt like repeating those feelings I had worked so hard to get past. As a child, I had to live in that house with him. But this was my home now. This was my safety zone. There would be no compromise here. Generosity had nothing to do with this. No, this was what I had to do to protect the home inside me.

In retrospect, I will tell you it was extremely painful for her. Not because I was nasty, accusing, hostile, or mean, but because I was very truthful. I had beaten her up with my feelings, but that wasn't the reason why I did it. It wasn't about revenge. I was just standing up for myself, and fighting for the right to my feelings.

Until this had been brought up with Melinda, I had never focused on it at all. Certainly, I had spent years overeating every time I was with my mom and Charles, but I never made the connection. I thought it was just the food. I always loved being with my mom and we were extremely close. Until Melinda gave me that shovel and we started going deeper, I never knew how much was there.

Watching my mom in pain was hard. But it also felt like the biggest weight off of me. I was so tired of carrying that bag. I would have continued to carry that load by myself if she hadn't accused me. Once she did, however, I needed her to take half of that junk and carry her own piece of luggage. After all, she was my mother. She's supposed to carry for me! That's exactly what it felt like.

I will never forget how she looked that day after we got back from our walk. Standing in the kitchen, Kleenex in hand, trying to regain her composure, she looked so wounded and tired. That was what I saw but that wasn't what I felt. What I felt was my resentment fading.

The day we took that walk was Bagel Day for our relationship. It opened up an honesty and it opened up some pain. But it also put things in perspective. My mom did not neglect me. My mom did not abuse me. She was never cruel, she's an upstanding person, and she's incredibly wise and perceptive. But she made some huge errors in how she handled some events that occurred in our lives. The emotional repercussions that I have to live with never go away. I've just learned how to manage them.

Was I right to tell her? In another time, with greater wisdom and maturity, I might have chosen otherwise. Had I chosen not to, though, I would have missed out on her response. My mom showed strength in all of her hurt. She cried but she told me not to fear her tears; she was all right. She expressed her own difficulty in what she had just heard from me. She questioned whether it was necessary for me to heap all this baggage on her and she felt some of her own anger at that. But she also understood. I didn't just respect her; it made me feel loved and heard.

Perhaps someone else could heal on her own, without ever involving the other person and dumping it in her lap. I wasn't able to do that. As you go through your own emotional rooms, your cleanup will be your own, having nothing to do with mine. Your decisions about how to clean them will come from your own place of comfort.

How did I get from resentment to a better place? I needed to remember that my mom had her own demons to fight in addition to raising two girls. Those unhappy events in my life were events in her life, too. As her daughter I couldn't see that then, but today it's important that I do.

I also need to hold on tight to the part of her that I admire. I need to see not what she didn't give but everything that she did. And I need to look at the good part of me that came from the good part of her.

My mom is devoted to things in their "natural state." She has a terrible distaste for falseness of any kind. She is not impressed by money or material things. When I was little she always insisted that I act "natural" and not show off or be coy. She always told me that although I was a slow learner, I had many untapped talents, and that one day they would come out.

My mom is so pretty, even now in her seventies. She has been complaining of wrinkles for years, but refuses to have plastic surgery. She never went in for fancy things or spending money just for show. I learned, from her, what I consider to be some pretty grounded values.

I learned inventive cooking from my mom. She has a knack for just throwing things together. While I am not as wide and practiced as she, I love to cook in that style. I also got my sense of appreciation from her. No matter what you give her, she lights up when she gets it. And when it comes to her view on most things in life, it is wise, centered, and true.

Today, there are times we are very close and very much connected. Other times we seem to be more distant. There are times I focus more on the disappointments that hurt, and other times I just enjoy her. I try not to judge her anymore, but I understand why I did. Not knowing her story, all I could see was my own. Without seeing her pain, all I could feel was my own.

I found a way to redirect the pain and use it to work on myself, especially when it comes to my kids. No matter how caught up I get in my emotions, on any given day, I work very hard to rise above it. I make sure my kids get what they need. I force myself out of my story and attempt to turn my attention to them. I also learned that having fun with them is the best distraction from pain. When I do that, we both win.

It's not like the bagel was fresh. It's not like my mom is perfect. It's not like I had to scrounge for food, and it's not like she doesn't love me. She loves me with all of her heart. Today I visit her and never visit her pantry. The need for the food there is gone.

Chapter 8

I stepped out of the room. I was back in the hallway. My hand was still on the knob. I gently turned it and let it go as soon as the lock engaged. Leaving a room, like the one with my mom, I was full of understanding. Surely this had to be it. Now the food would be gone. How devastating it felt when it wasn't. I had worked so hard and was getting tired. I wanted to get my paycheck. I wanted to lose ten pounds. I would have settled for five. Okay, fine, how 'bout two! One? A half? THROW ME A FREAKING BONE!

I was complaining a lot to Melinda. I felt like she couldn't help me. It wasn't her fault, I didn't blame her, but she just wasn't coming through. I did not give up on her. I did not quit our Tuesday housecleanings. But I told her I had found a way to feel safe and it was on a diet. I found a plan that was structured, gave me choices, and I actually liked the food. I'm not mentioning the plan by name because I can't say I recommend it. And I can't say I don't. It worked short-term and was what I needed at the time.

I'm bringing up this point because in your own work, you may feel points of frustration. What I believe in hindsight is that I needed to do two things at the same time. I definitely needed to work with Melinda. I needed to be consistent, dedicated, and committed to seeing it through. But there was a second part of my need at the time. I needed to feel safer with food while I waited to find long-term answers. Staying committed meant dealing with emotions, not food, which worked fine while I sat in her office. But what about when I was home, and faced the week with food? A structured eating plan was all that felt safe, and I thought a diet would provide that for me.

This had been a pattern with me for years. A diet was structured and clean. It gave me room to think about other things. A diet offered hope and felt exciting to me; it meant I couldn't gain weight. I didn't need to be afraid. A diet protected me from all bad things, the foods I couldn't control, and decisions I couldn't trust. I made sure not to touch even a morsel of food unless it was part of the program.

Usually, my discipline would last a week. Sometimes up to two weeks. One bite off the diet led to another. Once there was deviation, the diet was no longer safe. One step outside of a perfect record was all it took to lose it. Sometimes I would have a dream I was overeating and sabotaging the diet. I would wake up in a panic until I realized I hadn't done it. Phew! I was still safe; I hadn't blown it, still in that zone of safety.

Fearing her disapproval, I told Melinda I had started a diet. She told me that whatever made me feel safe was okay providing I made sure to eat. She let me know this was not what she recommended, but understood what I needed, and supported my decision. I began to lose weight right away. I was a very happy girl. I was working with Melinda, successfully dieting, and I believed I finally had it. Payday!

This time seemed different from my past attempts to diet and lose weight. Being in therapy and losing weight seemed to be the right combination. I remember walking into Melinda's office with a thinner body, and bellowing out these words: "See, this is the girl I was telling you about!" I was on top of the world.

I didn't tell Melinda but I felt a transfer of my trust. After all, my goal was to lose weight and that goal hadn't been reached until I started this diet. Melinda had let me down, but the diet had kept its promise. I trusted it more than her.

Then of course it happened. I just couldn't keep it up. There's only so long you can deprive your cravings. Separate from any emotional issues, I longed to have "real food." Real food meant a choice. Real food meant what I craved. If my diet said I couldn't have meat, meat was what I craved. If my diet said I couldn't have bread, bread was what I craved. If my diet said I couldn't have Tide, I would have licked the laundry. We all want what we can't have.

If being on a diet feels safe to you, there are definite pluses in that. Diets offer structure, portioning, and meals, and that's instrumental in taking off weight. If it's a good diet it will insist you eat regularly and will include foods that satisfy you. It will include lots of variety and let you make your own choices.

Just remember, a word of caution, diets don't deal with emotions. Nutritionists may talk about food plans, without regard to emotional eating. The more you deprive yourself of certain foods and disallow your cravings, the more you set yourself up to overeat. Of course, do what feels safe to you as you learn to connect eating to feelings.

You need to allow yourself imperfections. One day off or one bite off should be expected and accepted. If you beat yourself up, you will feel discouraged and then you'll turn to more food. If you find that you don't want or need to stay on a specific program, there is another approach to create more safety around food. Melinda insisted that structure was vital. She insisted that monitoring food in a journal was important as well. With that in mind, I came up with a method that always worked beautifully. I wrote up my own diet plan.

In the morning, or the night before, I would sit with a piece of paper. I would design a menu of what I would eat the next day. I would write down breakfast, snack, lunch, snack, dinner, and dessert. I would be very specific with measurements and amounts since that always felt safer to me. I would make sure the food was healthy enough, but I also made sure it was food I liked. I would allow two cookies or half a cup of frozen yogurt as a dessert.

This system worked so well for me, I could even eat with Scott. Sometimes it was the same food I made for him, and other times it wasn't. As long as the dinner that I would be eating was something I liked and wanted, I could often wait until he came home. If, however, I was getting too hungry, I ate before he came home.

As I went through the day, I would refer back to the sheet. I would draw a line through the foods as I ate them, eating them in the order of my mood at the time. Once I finished the food on the page, I felt closure to my eating. At that point or sometime later, I sat down to plan the next day. This felt huge to me. I loved the feeling of deciding what I wanted and planning for it, rather than, as I had done in the past, thinking about foods I wanted and figuring out how to avoid them.

If you don't know what foods to have or what calorie count would be right, here are several tips. You could ask your doctor. You could pick up a Weight Watchers plan. Or I'll give you some ideas up ahead. But try eating when you feel actual hunger and try stopping as you begin to feel full. Whatever you do, keep it safe. Keep it organized. Structure can be key to your initial success. Eating foods you like and enjoy is the key to your long-term endurance.

Chapter 9

Whenever I do a cleaning project in my house, and I'm speaking literally here, I love to look back at the work. If I organized my drawers, cleaned out my closet, or rearranged a room, I love to breeze past it with pride. I love a task completed. I can't say I've ever been a finisher in my life. I've started many job ventures, many projects, and not many were done to completion. There was truly only one thing in my life I could count on myself to finish. My plate.

For my housecleaning project on Tuesdays, it was different from doing my drawers. At home I could pull everything out, throw away the excess, and put the keepers back nice and neat. The very next day, I could marvel at my huge accomplishment. Not so fast on Tuesdays.

No, Tuesdays meant pulling every emotion out of a drawer and leaving it there, because something else demanded my attention. And because another drawer wouldn't close, I'd have to empty that one as well. I'd push something aside to make extra room and the whole drawer would end up collapsing. My insides were in disarray. I couldn't seem to finish in one place and then move on to another. There was never an end in sight.

If I were to describe this process in chronological exactness, I would have to do it in pieces. I would discuss an issue, go back to it, go back again, and then talk about how it feels today. Looking back, I can make some order of what was happening. I can even see it rationally. But emotions don't happen in rational order. They happen in messy drawers.

When I write about it now, it's presented in fast-forward. And in compartments that seem contained. I just need you to keep that in mind. Writing it is different than living it. Reading makes it sound smooth. It was anything but smooth.

About the same time I started with Melinda, I also started to run. I used to love to run a distance uphill, then look back and see the whole way behind me. Right now you're looking at the course I ran, but it looks smoother in the distance. I wasn't a professional runner. I had no idea how long, how far, or how hard the course would be. I just knew I was out for a run.

My hope is that your course will go a little smoother because you have someone who has a map. You'll be on your own, but you'll know it's possible to reach your destination. My point is that I started in the same place with no greater advantage than you. And while therapists can serve a vital role, they aren't necessarily runners. They may know how to treat a blister but can't always know how one feels. I can closely relate to the pain of that blister, especially when it pops open!

If I did it, anyone can. So let's pack up that first-aid kit and limp our way nice and easy. To grandmother's house we go.

Chapter 10

My grandmother's name was Mary. She passed away recently, six months shy of her one hundredth birthday. She was, no doubt, one of the stronger influences in my life. She was consistent. She was stubborn. She was generous and full of love. Two words that comes to mind when I describe my Nanny (pronounced "Nonny"; don't be calling her Nanny) are *the same.* Nanny was the same.

She cooked the same dishes over and over. They were always delicious. She repeated the same phrases over and over. "It ain't funny, McGee!" She always said the same thing to the owner of a nearby boutique when she walked through the door. "I need everything," she'd say. After she tried everything on, exhausting me and the salesperson, she'd say the same thing as she left empty-handed. "I don't need anything right now. When do I ever go out?"

My parents divorced amicably when I was seven. Until the time my sister, Laurie (she's Laura now; don't be calling her Laurie), and I left home for college, my dad kept a consistent schedule with us. Wednesday nights we went to Nanny's for dinner. Friday nights we had dinner at my dad's apartment. Not quite the cook he would become later in life, we always had steak and baked beans.

Every Sunday he picked us up for the day. He took us to movies, children's plays, ice-skating, picnics, friends' homes, water skiing, snow skiing, and weekends in the country.

My grandmother lived on the eighteenth floor of a high rise on Chicago's Lake Shore Drive. Going up the elevator, around the fourteenth floor, I'd begin to smell her cooking. Nanny's was a place where buckles would have to be loosened. Wednesday was an eating night.

When we complained about her slipcovers peeling the skin off our legs, she always had the same answer. "When you stop wearing jeans, I'll take them off." We sat in her dining room under her big chandelier, my dad, my sister, my uncle Herbie (it's Herb; don't be . . .), and me. Herbie is an uncle by title, but quite a bit more in heart. He is strong and handsome and reminds me of Gregory Peck. He reminds Scott and me of Spencer Tracy in the movie *Guess Who's Coming to Dinner*. And he came to dinner every Wednesday. He has a way of talking that commands attention wherever he goes. His voice is strong and loud. One of my kids once described him perfectly. "Uncle Herbie talks like he really means it."

Sometimes during the summer, our Wednesday night dinners would be spent on Herbie's boat. Nanny would bring her chopped liver. Herbie would cook up some steaks. Later, after we finished eating, we would cruise along the Chicago River. While everyone else (sometimes my great-aunts came, too) stayed inside down below, my dad huddled with Laurie and me. We sat on top, toward the front of the boat, as the water sprayed and chilled us. These were my favorite Wednesdays. When we'd just cuddle and look at the skyline. I never focused on the food on the boat, only the white lights that sat near the water's edge, lighting the Wrigley Building up like a castle.

The white lights under the chandelier, however, were quite a different experience. The talk at the table was often politics, which I knew nothing about. My sister and Herbie had strong opinions, and loud discussions would always take place. Laurie was on the left. Herbie was on the right. I am not referring to where they were sitting, either! While they argued about Republicans and Democrats, I went for second helpings. Unfortunately, Nanny had carefully calculated how much each person would eat, and cooked to that exact quantity. One veal chop each for Laurie and me. One veal chop for Nanny. Two veal chops each for my dad and Herbie. Nanny didn't like leftovers.

When I got bored during dinner with discussions I knew nothing about, and there were no more veal chops to be had, I would disappear into the bathroom. Nanny had a three-way mirror and I would put my face inside it. I would put my finger over the bump on my nose and check out the new, improved profile. I wanted to see what that honker would look like if the bump could ever be gone. I did this every Wednesday. When I returned to the table, Nanny would be upset. "Why does she get up in the middle of dinner every single week? I think she eats too fast. The food goes right through her!"

Dessert would finally come. She usually baked strudel cookies and apricot-filled horns. If we decided to take one or two cookies, Nanny wouldn't complain. If she saw me taking more than that, she would give me a slap on the hand. If we didn't eat at least one, she would holler, "Everyone's on a diet!"

The Wednesday nights of my childhood were the most consistent part of my life. With the closest family ties. With the strongest personalities. Nanny's life was her family. My dad was dependable in his commitment and time. Herbie was steadfast in his strength and involvement. Each of them formed the backbone of my very existence, though I never realized it at the time.

Wednesday night dinners continued again after I returned home from college. But often I visited Nanny during the week by myself. We had light and healthy meals together when it was just the two of us. She frustrated me at times; I used to get very angry at her lack of flexible thinking. We would have a fight, get it out, and when it was done it was done.

After I got married and had kids, I visited Nanny at least once a week with them. I loved seeing her with them, the sense of history, of generations, and I knew it made her so proud. She looked years younger the second she saw their faces. We would spend time in her den, where she would coo and eat them up. While she did this, I would go into the kitchen, find her graham crackers, and I would eat *them* up. Before arriving, I knew I'd be paying them a visit. We had a once-a-week thing.

Melinda had a phrase that she used quite often. "Sit with the feelings." Figure out what the feeling is, separate it from the food, and sit with it. What was I feeling at Nanny's? Was this a sign of some deep, dark skeleton of my complicated relationship with her? Nope, this one was pretty simple. I didn't like sharing her. When the kids were there, her attention was turned completely to them. Oh, cut me some slack. I didn't say I was proud of that, and I don't compete with my kids. But I still like my attention. So shoot me.

Today I recognize that divided attention is hard for me. Being at Nanny's while she played with the kids was making me feel left out. The political arguments with Herbie and Laurie had also left me out. I needed to find a way to get involved or learn to sit with the boredom. I needed to find something to do, without occupying myself with food.

When I went to the hospital to see Nanny the last time before she died, she didn't move. She didn't open her eyes and she didn't speak at all. She hadn't spoken in weeks. But I was captivated even so. I looked at her hands, which I knew so well. I looked at her beautiful hair. Here was this woman who had loved me all my life. All she ever wanted was for me to be happy; she had said it so many times. She had also told me there was nothing more important than family. She had said that so many times, too.

She always talked about dying. She wanted me to have her pearls. I once asked her what I would do without her. How would I ever get through it? She said, "Sweetheart, you'll have the memories and that will be enough."

I walked up to the railing on her bed, leaned down, and whispered in her ear, even though I knew she couldn't answer, "Nanny, I love you." And right away, without hesitation, she told me she loved me, too. The last words she ever spoke. No prepared dishes, no talk of politics, no undoing my button. Just a quiet room full of memories and once again she was right. That would be enough.

Chapter 11

I'm a little bit concerned. Maybe a tad self-conscious. You may be wondering, amid all this food-obsessing, how did I live my life? Well, that's what made it all so confusing. My life went along quite well, particularly my adulthood. I will tell you, so you don't think I'm completely gone, that there were four times in my life when I had no problems with food whatsoever. Four time periods when my eating was normal, I didn't obsess about food, and my weight was not an issue.

One was the year of my engagement. I didn't obsess the whole year. Two was the birth of my daughter. I didn't obsess for at least a month. Three was the birth of my first son, and four was the birth of my second son. Plus vacations; I never had food issues on vacations. Ha-ha, that makes five. See how normal I was?

Here is some chronological history. After my parents got divorced, our house on the south side of Chicago was sold, and we moved into an apartment on the north side. My sister and I transferred to different schools. I had left all of my friends, but found new ones very quickly. There were two girls my age in our building.

After the move, I developed a dependency on my mom and freaked out every time she left. If I knew she was going out on a Saturday night, I cried all afternoon. I begged her not to go. Even on the days I was to be with my dad, I was homesick for my mom. My comfort was with her and with being at home.

I was very self-conscious and insecure. Most of my friends lived in houses in nicer neighborhoods and their parents were married. Financially, my dad was totally responsible for us and he was as generous as he could afford to be. But we didn't live with him, and my mom was more strapped for money. I always envied those who had more than we had.

Three years later, when I was ten, my mom married Charles. My sister and I, as I said before, had no relationship with him at the time. He knew we were close with our dad and kept his distance with respect to that. My sister was very removed from us; I hardly ever saw her, except when we went with my dad. From that time on there was a separateness to the way we all lived together. I felt lonely and depressed. We were just coexisting.

My life became my friends. I was never popular, I didn't consider myself all that pretty, and I always felt kind of big. When I wasn't overweight, I thought I was. I was cursed with very small friends! I knew that I was unhappy so I devised my own survival. Yellow. I decorated my room in yellow as an island amid the gray.

Overeating and bingeing for me began in high school and stayed with me until I got help, which wasn't until my midthirties. There were periods, as I said, when bingeing was less of a problem and periods when it was more. The worst it ever got was about five years into my marriage. More about that later.

During my high school years, overeating was more of a problem than bingeing, and to be thin was always my wish. I ate a lot every day after school. I ate a lot on Saturday nights. I ate without restraint, which is why I didn't binge. By my junior year I was almost thirty pounds heavier than I am today. I would try different diets, sometimes with my friends. I don't remember them working until my senior year. I had my first boyfriend and my weight dropped maybe ten pounds.

In college I began to bloom. I felt more confidence in myself. I had overcome a terrible homesickness, and found my place with friends. My sophomore year I became close friends with a girl and we spent all our time together. We had bingeing down to a science.

We were about the same weight. We could both have stood to lose a couple, but we were not considered to be heavy. Not at all. We even did some modeling together.

I remember some pretty crazy diets we did, and we'd exchange daily reports of food and weight. One was a banana, hot dog, and hard-boiled egg diet. We would spend a few days on a diet, lose a few pounds, and then have our ritual binge: Domino's Pizza with onions (only), an entire bag of Rich 'n Chips, and our Diet Sunkist. And popcorn. Lots and lots of air-popped popcorn.

One day she wasn't feeling well, I think she had cramps, and she wasn't all that hungry. So I went to McDonald's, got Quarter Pounders with cheese, fries, and Diet Cokes. We weren't quite satisfied, so we called Domino's and ordered a large pizza. There was one additional problem; she had to have something sweet after something salty. I went to Baskin-Robbins to buy an ice cream cake. Finally, her cramps were better but we couldn't get up from the couch. Literally.

Were we unhappy? We would never have described ourselves that way. We had a close, fun, and trusting friendship. I'm not even sure we questioned all of our eating; it was just something we did. I felt happy and enjoyed my life. I had a boyfriend who I simply adored. But I was struggling more with school and worrying about my grades.

Here is my moment of truth; do I write about this or skip over it? At the time it was so devastating and a secret only two people knew about, my girlfriend and my boyfriend. I know what you're thinking and that's not it. It was something entirely different. Okay, here goes.

It happened during my junior year. I was a journalism major with a concentration in advertising and a minor in psychology. My grades were average to just above. I had poor study habits and trouble with some of the courses. Except for journalism. I loved the advertising classes and longed to be a copywriter one day. My favorite class was with Dr. Burton, a retired advertising executive from Leo Burnett, the biggest agency in Chicago. He was known to never give A's and was ridiculously tough on assignments. I admired him more than any professor I had ever known and I loved, loved, loved his class.

We got an assignment to write an ad for a moped. This was when they had just come out. He told us to write two separate ads; one should be light, fun, and clever, and the other was to be more hard-sell. I came up with my two ads. My clever one showed a guy on a moped on a warm sunny day with the headline above: SUN-ROOF INCLUDED. The second, my hard-sell ad, showed a woman on the moped with a basket on the back full of groceries and assorted bags. That headline read: RUN 100 ERRANDS ON ONE GAL-LON OF GAS. I earned an A and he held my ads up in class as an example of what he wanted. Understand, I was never an A student. I could never keep up with my classes. This for me was a moment in time. I had never been so proud.

My nightmare class was news broadcasting and we were graded on our attendance. I showed up for every class. I knew better than to miss them since I found the subject so difficult. We were graded on performance mostly inside the class. We were given news off the wires as they would have come into the station. We had to write for a broadcast in a very concise and uniform manner. We were timed and under the gun. There was no room for extra words or personal style here. That kind of writing was so difficult for me. I simply couldn't do it.

I was concerned about my grade. I went to talk to my professor. I needed to get above a C in the class or it wouldn't apply toward my major. He told me not to worry; if I got a B on the final, I would get a B in the class. The final was two-thirds of the grade. The day of the final came. We were given sheet after sheet of news material that needed to be typed for a broadcast. I was over-whelmed and I cracked. This was not a test to study for; it was an on-the-spot performance. He flunked my final and gave me a D+ in the class. I would not graduate on time.

I couldn't believe he would do this. It's not like I hadn't tried. I had gone to all the classes, shown concern for my grade, and done the best I could. I went to my counselor, who felt bad for me but said there was nothing she could do. I should have gone to see him. I should have fought the grade. Instead I just let it go, and left to go home for the summer.

The next semester, the first of my senior year, I started out with a full schedule. I didn't feel I could take on an extra class, to make up for the failed one. I suppose I felt defeated and depressed knowing I would not graduate with my friends, and would have to stay on for summer school after everyone left. Gradually, without a true awareness, subject by subject I gave up attending my classes. I was falling further and further behind.

Every day and every week was another day and week I lost. I wanted to get back on track but it felt hopeless and impossible. There was just no way to catch up. It was a horrifying secret. I felt like I was living a lie. I watched my friends with their studying and classes and I felt so left out of life. I was going to fail every class if I didn't turn this around.

I felt the semester slip from my hands. I was wasting my dad's money and he had no idea what was happening. I couldn't bear to tell anyone. Every day I waited for my roommate to come home from her classes, envying her normal school life. I was sitting out, lonely and depressed, not knowing what I could do. That semester I failed every class and I never went back to finish. I never graduated college. A secret that I still carry and one most of my friends don't know. There goes the résumé!

I believe to this day that it was not the issue of graduating on time that led to the nightmare of that semester. I believe it was two things. One was my inability to voice my feelings to the instructor and fight for a higher grade. The one I felt I deserved. The other was my inability to confront what was happening instead of waking up each day to the lie. I should have gone to someone. I should have crawled out of my shame. Instead I crawled into a hole. I'm not sure I ever really crawled out, until I made the choice to tell you.

I was afraid to tell my parents. Not confronting the situation caused me to sit out of my life. Stuffing myself with pizza distracted me from my pain. I couldn't face an instructor who failed me. That's how I failed myself.

Here's a Hollywood example of the power of distraction. Did you see the movie *Die Hard: With a Vengeance* with Bruce Willis? Don't you just love that guy? Anyway, the bad guys planned to steal billions from a government storage vault. To distract all the cops and feds from the site, they put out devastating bomb threats. They made the police believe that schools, malls, and downtown areas were all targets to be blown up. The bomb threats weren't real. They were simply there as a distraction, while the money got carried out.

Food obsessions are bomb threats that distract us from the feelings that are threatening. The more we fight the food, the further we are from the truth. The food is a deliberate decoy to keep our focus from what we're avoiding. How many times have you faced a tedious chore and gone to get food instead? It's no different with emotions.

Those food threats are in restaurants, in other people's houses; they are every place we go. That's because our feelings are with us every place we go. Just remember, we are the ones creating the food threats, and then we chase them down. Would Bruce Willis chase his own tail? Maybe for twenty million a picture. But we don't get paid nearly enough, for all the chasing we do.

Everyone who knows me knows that I have a thing about honesty. They would probably welcome a lie from me like a week in the South of France. There are times I should keep my big mouth shut and learn to keep it inside. But I don't. This probably came from two places.

One was my college nightmare, and the pain of all that hiding. The other was my training with regard to eating. I spent so much time learning to uncover my feelings, the ones that were true and honest, that any breach of that seems like a breach of my soul. Living against what I feel, or lying about what I do, is next to impossible for me. I pay a high price for it and so does everyone else. But it just happens to be who I am.

My family, my friends, and mostly my husband have been on the receiving end of my brutal and painful truths. They would tell you that there's no bigger pain in the ass than me and they wouldn't wish my thoughts on their worst enemy. They would tell you that they wish I would be a little less honest and hold a little more inside. And sometimes my honesty does damage. I know they've all heard more than they wanted to and on more than one occasion. But I believe they would also tell you that our relationships are deep and compelling. Genuine, pure, and connected. They sure as hell are not boring. And above all they are honest. As honest as honest can be.

Once you realize what the threat is, that it's as simple as your feelings inside, you won't have to be so afraid. All the truth does is put your options on the table. The truth just gives information that allows you to make knowing choices. Decisions are yours to make. If it's honest it may be hurtful. But if it's honest it may also help. If it's honest it may cause anger. So what. We're all entitled to anger if that's our response to the truth.

Secrets are tough. Living a lie is the loneliest form of being alone. It's not just being alone. It's being alone with a liar. Food is a nonjudgmental companion, but it's no substitute for the truth. Or for a relationship. Whatever my relationships are or aren't, I need them to be honest. Full of emotion, scary as hell, but based on fact, not fiction. Well, that's the way I like it. Pain in the ass that I am.

Chapter 12

"Will you be nursing?" she asked. "Yes," I said. Scott looked at me like he was in the wrong room. I had vowed to all who tried to talk me into nursing that I would not be. It seemed kind of weird to me. But when the nurse handed me my daughter I decided that any part of my body that would attach to hers was all right by me. I had no idea what love like that would feel like.

Food did not interest me. I could have cared less about my body except for what it could provide to her. I wanted to eat healthfully. I wasn't just me anymore; I was a lifeline to that baby girl. There was no obsessing. There were no self-image concerns. There was no worrying about feeling safe, only making sure that she was.

When I woke up in the morning she was the first thing I thought of; not avoiding breakfast, not how fat I was or how thin I needed to be. Certainly I wanted to lose the weight I had gained, which ended up being more than forty pounds. Pregnancy had been a free ride with food. Once I bought a bucket of rib tips to eat in the car. That was on the way to dinner! But now I had my baby and food was no longer the focus. Spreading a freshly washed, soft, pink blanket on top of my bed and watching the way her nose moved when she breathed; that was what guided my thoughts. I had never felt so content in my life.

Just over two years later, I lay waiting for Scott to return to my room. He had gone to the children's hospital where our son had been taken the day before, the same day he was born. I wasn't expecting bad news. We weren't led to believe the problem was too serious. It was. Scott walked into the room, and when I looked at his face, I knew something was terribly wrong. "We have a very sick baby," he told me. And with that he started to cry. The baby's kidneys weren't functioning and the doctors said he might not make it. With his specific condition, they weren't offering much hope. They told Scott that the quality of his life, at best, would be abnormal. They said we might need to make the decision whether or not to save him. I felt the life being sucked out of me.

I got up from the bed. The only words I spoke were "We need to go and see him." I was determined to get to that hospital. I was in shock and couldn't speak. I put on my clothes and walked past some of our family members who had gotten the news from Scott and had rushed there to be with us. I couldn't look to them for comfort; I could only look past them. I knew if I stopped or faced their eyes, I would never get to my son.

I walked into the neonatal intensive care unit, a large room with about six babies including our son. I hadn't cried yet. I was on some sort of autopilot; my destination had been that room. I put on the gown, walked over to the side of the crib, and my body just bent forward and folded. I threw out cries from somewhere in the middle of my stomach and just let it all come out. He looked so small in this room. He was hooked up to various things and I had no idea what they were. Somewhere in the midst of my sobbing I became aware of someone behind me. Gently and quietly a nurse came up and spoke to me very softly. "Excuse me, Mrs. Goodman," she said as she pointed across the room. "That's your son over there." Oh.

I walked over to my son. He was so healthy-looking. He was so big, and his hands were so large and strong. He looked too good to have something so terribly wrong with him. I stared down at that beautiful baby who we had teased about being ugly the day before. I leaned over his face and looked at him. Suddenly my crying stopped. I no longer felt so afraid. I proceeded to give him his first instructions, mother to son, out loud. I felt something different after seeing him. It wasn't my own strength I sensed. The strength

I sensed was his. I said to him, "You have to make yourself better. You have to work very hard and be very strong. I know you can do it."

That day Scott and I left the hospital. The doctor had suggested I take something so I could get some sleep and we stopped at the grocery store to fill the prescription. Scott walked into the store while I waited in the car. I remember watching the people in the parking lot and wishing I could be one of them. I imagined an ordinary grocery list. Life as we knew it was over. I felt like I was in a trance.

That night our family came over. Our two-year-old daughter was staying with my sister-in-law and she didn't know any of this. Scott and I were glued together. When we went to bed that night, we didn't know what to hope for. But we made a united decision. Not saving him would not be an option.

The next day, we had an appointment to see the specialist. Before seeing him, the doctors told us that our son's kidney function had dramatically improved but they didn't say anything more. We met with the specialist in a big conference room, ready to hear all bad things. He asked us what we'd been told. We told him and he shook his head. "I'm sorry you had to go through that. Your son will be just fine." What? WHAT? He explained our son's condition. He said that the doctors' prognosis had been wrong in our son's case. He would live a normal life. As a matter of fact, we could take him home in a few days.

Scott was in shock, not really believing, and doubting what he was hearing. I jumped out of my chair. With complete trust and total belief, my celebration began. "It's the miracle we thought could never be!" I had heard all I needed to hear. Our baby would be just fine. There were health issues to deal with. Great, fine, I'm okay with all that, just let me go see my baby.

Immediately I went back to see him. "Good boy, you did such a good job!" I really felt like he had listened. Today he never does. Well, eventually he listens after maybe ten or eleven times. And you'll never hear me complain. And how I still love his hands.

During that period of time, and after we brought him home, food was not a part of my life. I ate enough to stay healthy but I didn't have much of an appetite. We had been through a lot and we were celebrating our good fortune. We felt like we had lived a nightmare and then been handed a miracle. Funny thing about miracles; they take your mind off food.

My daughter's birth was the unique experience of the firstborn child. The disbelief, the magic, the amazement, and the 100 percent focus you put on every tiny move or sound he or she makes. With a first child there is no such thing as insignificant. Food couldn't compete with that.

My son's birth was what my husband and I refer to as "the gift." Fearing the loss of him and having gone through such a life-altering event, we were forced to see life differently. He brought us perspective. He brought us everything good. Not a day goes by that we don't appreciate everything differently because of him. When he was born, food couldn't compete with that either.

Five years later, a year after I stopped seeing Melinda, I gave birth to what would be my last baby. I'm not sure what it was about this third-born second son, and first time it felt so easy. I was giddy with joy. I was so connected to this child. I wanted nothing more than to be with him. It was not a secret I kept from my two older kids. As a matter of fact, I intentionally pointed out all the things about him that were so over-the-top cute so they could enjoy it along with me. We all fell in love with that baby. We shared our joy together, so jealousy was not an issue. Food wasn't an issue either.

The births of each of my children represented three of the five times I mentioned I had no issues with food. When I say "no issues" I mean that food was not number one in my thoughts. I ate, I enjoyed, I was conscious of my weight. But I didn't make it my life. And it wasn't something I feared.

In order to understand where your eating obsessions come from, you also need to understand where they don't come from. You need to learn where you feel safe with food and notice where there's less of that focus. Those are the places where you are comfortable and being true to yourself. Understand what a critical point this is; where there is no food-obsessing there is no lie. There is nothing tearing you away from you. It doesn't mean there's no pain. It simply means there's no lie.

When my babies were born, the love was so pure and intense. I had never experienced anything like it. I felt an attachment that was deep to my core and I felt necessary to someone's survival. It was perfect love. Now that they're older it still feels that perfect, even on the days they don't need me. I never feel voids with my kids, because the inside of "us" feels full.

When you find yourself in a situation where your inside feelings don't match your outside behavior, or you're in a relationship that leaves you unfull, that can become a food trap. These "food traps" come up all the time and you've not yet learned how to avoid them. I've got a weapon for you to protect yourself. Once you learn how to use it, you'll no longer find yourself captured. Use this as your mantra:

SAFE

Separate Always Food and Emotion

Chapter 13

The fire alarm has gone off in your home. The beeping is loud and piercing. You check upstairs, you don't smell smoke, but you know it went off due to something. So you search your house for the cause.

I want you to stop thinking of your eating issues as a curse and start thinking of them as an alarm. Every time they go off they are warning you of emotional smoke, and here there are no false alarms. You will learn to use your eating issues as the best protection you have against burning emotions. Be thankful you have this alarm. It will save you time after time.

This is a system I use all the time when I need to assess dangerous places in relation to food. I literally check in on my "food thoughts" with nearly every decision I make. If the alarm goes off, I know something is up within that decision or event. Remember SAFE. It works. It has become as automatic as checking my calendar. Here's how you "Separate Always Food and Emotion."

Think of food obsessions, food fears, or weight concerns as the beep. It's warning you that there is emotional discomfort or upheaval. What you're looking at is your reaction. For example, you get invited to a get-together. Is there any food thought built into your response? Or, let's say you just hung up the phone after talking to someone; anyone. Immediately you find yourself reaching for food or worrying about food.

In your everyday life, there are people and events that cause you to feel unsettled inside. That means you feel uncomfortable with the emotions brought on by a person or situation. It is here that food gets "played out," as Melinda would say. In order to try to help you see it, let's write it down.

Take two sheets of paper. Write "SAFE" on top of one, and "Not SAFE" on top of the other. Hey, I just had a better idea; I'll do it for you. At the end of this chapter, I'll leave two blank pages with the headings. I'll even give you some examples of where I am SAFE and Not SAFE. Then you can fill in with yours.

Write down as many people and situations as you can think of. When deciding whether they're SAFE or Not SAFE, imagine yourself there and try to tap into what it feels like. Do you imagine feeling anxious or do you feel comfortable and relaxed? SAFE means you don't feel anxious about food. Not SAFE means you do. It's possible everything right now feels unsafe. That's okay. It won't stay that way much longer.

In addition, as I did with the birth of my children, recall events in your past where food was not a primary concern. Or activities you participate in that don't revolve around food or a desire for food. This could include shopping, working, gardening, exercising, organizing, reading, projects, etc. Where was food an issue? And where did it lose its power? Think of anything at all, even something you've never done, where food would be second choice.

It could be a person you'd spend time with. It could be someone you've never met but would like to. It could be a class you've been longing to take. A place you've wanted to go. Or maybe it's just sitting somewhere quiet, away from the noise of the day. What would be more interesting than food? Use your imagination. These images should come not only from what is in your life today. They should come from what is not.

The next part is crucial and extremely revealing. Take a separate sheet of paper for this one. You're going to list all the people you associate with, including spouse, boyfriends, girlfriends, friends, children, parents, siblings, grandparents, coworkers, bosses, employees, former crushes, best friends, people you dislike, or people who work in your home. Imagine yourself around these people. What do you see happening with food? Write it down; SAFE or Not SAFE?

The last thing to look at is whether you seem to focus on food more when you're alone or when you're around other people. Do you avoid eating with others and eat the minute you're alone? Do you eat around others and feel less compelled to eat when you're alone? Here are some examples of places to wave your meter. Food thoughts are your indicator. Where do food issues seem to be high and denser? Take a pen and write it down below.

1. Your home. What is the difference in your eating while you're home by yourself as opposed to when others are with you? What time of the day seems to be easier; when do you feel less in control?

2. Your job at various points of the day. Does late afternoon send off the signals? Are there things that go on at work that always seem to be difficult with regard to your eating? List them.

3. Your neighbor's house. Do you find yourself thinking about the food there?

4. Your in-laws' house or being in their company. What happens with food?

5. Your parents' home or presence. Do you always overeat there? Do you forget about food there?

6. A party (your own or somewhere else). Are food fears here? Do you worry about what you'll be able to eat? Do you worry about what you'll weigh? Or does the party become what you focus on and you look forward to the day it arrives? Describe the last party you went to and what happened with the food. Who was there?

7. Dinner out with your spouse, date, friend, etc. What are these dinners like? Do you obsess about where you'll meet, what kind of food is served, and how you'll avoid the bread? Describe some examples.

8. Waiting. Oh, my gosh, that's a tough one. Think about all the parts of your day and life that require you to wait. You're all ready to be picked up. The person you're waiting for is late. Later. You're frustrated and angry, so here's what we need to know. Do you go to food? Describe a recent wait.

What about at the restaurant? You're waiting for your food. You're hungry. There are breadsticks on the table. Can you wait for your meal to come and engage in conversation? Or do you have to eat what's there? Gotcha! Write it down.

Waiting for an answer. It will be days until you find out. Anything from a job offer to a house offer, or whether some plans are on. You are waiting for some news. During that time, whether it's hours, days, or weeks, what's going on with your eating?

9. Vacation. Does this change your eating in any way? Better or worse? And judge also by the person you are with. Write about the last one.

10. Exercising. What does the actual doing or thinking about doing bring up for you? Do you eat less when you exercise? Do you eat more since you already burned calories, entitling you to more food? Or does the thought make you eat, merely as a diversion from getting down to do something you so terribly dread? I'll leave extra space for this one!

11. Shopping. What happens to food thoughts when you shop? Does some shopping cause a problem while other shopping does not? Does a day of shopping send you on

stops for nibbles here and there or does it so consume your time that you could skip food altogether?

12. Eating. Yep, eating. What kind of eating triggers food issues for you? What kind of eating feels safer? Are there certain foods you need to stay away from? Foods you can't feel control around? It seems that most people have food that they say they can't have around. What foods are they, and what do they cause you to do? These are foods you'll look at later when we go to stock your kitchen.

As you make your own list, visualize each place or person. Create a scene around it. For example, imagine yourself on a private terrace, overlooking a beach where no one else is around. You are allowed to stay one hour. You have something you brought to read if you want to or you could just close your eyes and drift off. It's just a little cool, so you're wearing new cozy sweats. It's private and quiet and you are sitting in the shade or the sun. Food is available with easy access if you so desire but it's not sitting right in front of you. Would you need it right away? Would you feel bored by this and need something more to do? Or would it be so relaxing and all you would need, for one perfect hour?

Here's another scene: You are meeting someone for lunch. You are waiting in the restaurant. Walk yourself through lots of people choices and imagine your feeling as you watch each person enter and sit down to join you. And let's just imagine you are not starving but mildly hungry for lunch. Are there certain people you know who would cause you to eat more than others?

Arrange a party in your mind. Pick out some guests to invite. Are there some who make you think of grabbing a plate? Is there someone you hope won't show up? Who comes to the party and always brings along food thoughts? Boring people? People you don't like? People who make you uneasy? Food tells many stories. Start to read the one that is yours.

Picture yourself in a job. Is there one that makes you eat more than another? Don't be fooled by the obvious. There are plenty of people working in restaurants and bakeries who don't overeat while they're there. And there are people in offices who keep stashes in their desks, or pig out when they go to lunch. Focus on the work; what interests you, captures you? What job would be your dream? What would be more gratifying than food?

You're on vacation with your spouse. Eating or not eating?

You're on vacation with your friends. Eating or not eating?

You're on vacation by yourself. Eating or not eating?

Separate food from emotion. Separate food from events. Where do you want to be? Who do you want to be with? What would you like to do? What would you rather sit out of? What can you do without? What must be a part of your life? Who makes you feel uncomfortable? Who makes you come alive? *Tap, tap, tap. Bang, bang, bang. Crunch, crunch, crunch.* What is all that noise? Let's find out, shall we?

SAFE

A few personal examples:

1. A specific girlfriend comes to mind. I never overeat when I'm with her alone.
2. My house by myself. I rarely overeat when I'm alone there. Quiet time in my house is a commodity more precious than food.
3. My uncle Herbie's house in Florida. I never overeat when I'm with him.
4. Writing. I never need food when I sit down to do any kind of writing. If I get up because I'm hungry, I have something worth returning to, so the food doesn't go on and on.

Not SAFE

1. Another specific girlfriend. I always eat more when I'm with her.
2. My house when the kids come home after school. Troops invading the peace.
3. Last day of vacation. The transition is tough for me.
4. Showers or luncheons. I don't like them unless they are thrown for me!

Chapter 14

An old baby-sitter of ours named Anne, who's become kind of a younger sister to me, was visiting us recently. She was telling me about her job. She works for a woman who has a four-year-old daughter, is somewhere between her third and fourth husband, and works full-time and then some. She's hired many different sitters over the course of her daughter's life; no one seems to stay.

It's not a big surprise that this little girl is a handful. She's clingy, needy, temperamental, and never wants to go out. Not even to the park. Anne was telling me that it's a great job because the pay is good, she has full use of a car, and, after all, it's only one child. Her only problem is that she seems to put on weight whenever she is working. Do you see where I'm going here?

She described her workday as an all-day fight not to eat. All she can think about is what her next snack should be and she can't wait for it to be mealtime. As she drives the girl to school, all she can think about is what she will eat, what she shouldn't eat, and how she can get through this day without food.

I suggested that perhaps her job was boring her, frustrating her, and not giving her any room to create. Food had become something to occupy her, interest her, and something to give some thought to. She needed to make a choice.

I told her that jobs can be boring. It doesn't mean you quit them and you may not see that as an option. It doesn't mean you stay either. It means you make a decision; a knowing, understanding, responsible, sound decision. If your decision is to stay, you sit with the feeling of boredom and find something within that situation to make it more creative.

I suggested that maybe the true challenge here was to make a positive impact on this little girl. Maybe she could initiate a turning point for the girl, become someone she later remembers as having made a difference in her childhood. Of course there is a second option: Find another job. Just know it comes down to choice. Not a choice of what to eat; a choice of what to do.

Jobs are one kind of boring. People are another. Raising kids can get a bit tiring. Relationships and marriage, give me a break. How much more boring can they get? Eating fills those moments and days. Then something happens worse than all of that boredom. We become bored with ourselves.

But when we take ourselves away from the food, and pour that energy someplace else, we become more interesting people. We have more to bring to those jobs and relationships and everything starts to feel different. Ever stop to think that maybe it's not the relationship or job that's so boring? Ever consider it might be you?

Let's start a competition of interest. It's food versus you; so put up your dukes and fight. Let's see who comes out on top. Today it may be the food. Tomorrow . . . the title just may be yours. And the new lightweight champion *is* . . .

Chapter 15

It was 95 degrees outside. The air was still and heavy. My little guy's temperature stood just a little above the temperature outside; about 101 and coughing. This would be a long day. I knew I'd better get some exercise to pump energy into my day. I had a sitter and that was lucky; I could get out for an hour.

On the days I don't have a sitter, and don't have that break in the day, I make sure to structure my food. Sometimes I welcome the time at home. Other days I feel like a horse in a stall and I just want to get out and run. On those days, particularly if I know ahead of time that I will be in all day, I will get up very early, I'm talking five-thirty, and get some exercise before Scott leaves for work. I may wait until he comes home later. After a long day at home, even if I'm tired, working out gives me the break that I need.

This day, my friends stayed in, no one wanted to take a walk or run; it was just too hot to do anything. Since they decided to sit it out, that gave me my chance; I went out and had a great run. Anyone can walk or run in seventy degrees. Anyone can survive a happy day. When life gets hot and feels like hell, now, that's when you go out and prove yourself. That's when you make yourself strong. Son of a bitch, fucking A, that's when you see what you're made of.

During that run I thought of you. I began writing this book with a sole purpose: to somehow get through to people with similar problems as I've had. I felt that if I could give one person some encouragement, or help someone get to a better place with eating issues, it would all be worthwhile. But something else has happened. I like connecting with you.

Outside of my family and my routine, I have found this place to go. It's you. I like you. I find you a lot more interesting than the food I used to think about. And what makes you so interesting? How should I know? We've never met. I don't know your name, or what you look like, and I don't know where you live. I don't know what your days are like, or whether you sleep well at night.

Everywhere I go now, I'm thinking about things I want to say to you. I find analogies to make my points. I'm remembering where I was, what I needed to know, and how hopeless I felt inside. I remember how alone I felt, never having spoken with someone who survived this. In my mind, I am telling you the things I needed to hear myself, when I was in that place you are in now.

For a wife and mother without a job outside the home, food and diet gives a sense of purpose. It's not that we don't love what we do, but often we long for more. We feel trapped by time and logistics. Or kids with sore throats and fevers. Physically and emotionally when we long for more, food is something to have. It's easy, it's fast, and it's always there. We know we need to replace the food; what we don't know is what could replace it.

This would be no different from someone who does work but the job has become routine. There is a longing for something greater in life but there's no time or ability to find it. Food is an escape from the work. Food relieves the stress. Food is a break from monotonous hours and responsibility that feels like too much. But again, where would we look for more?

I used to envy women who worked but resented them for "leaving" their kids, unless they needed the income. I wasn't in that position; my husband earned enough money. I would look at thin working women and say to myself, "Oh, sure, I would be skinny, too, if I had a life!" Don't get me wrong. I wanted to be home with my kids and I loved the life that I had. I just needed something that would make me feel some challenge and excitement.

Here's what I believe today. "Leaving" your kids is exactly what you do with obsessions. Even when you are physically there your mind is someplace else, and you are not with your kids that way either.

Before I started writing this book, I told my kids of my plan. I explained that it would be taking some of my time and I wanted them to understand that. I told them how much this meant to me but of course they were far more important. I explained there would be chunks of time I would be writing, but if ever they felt they needed me, or needed more attention, they would have to let me know. I have yet to get that tap on the shoulder. But I am getting something else.

As the pages begin to accumulate and I see a book taking form, I feel a new sense of purpose. I feel energy, and guess where that goes? It goes straight to my kids. I am more fun. I laugh harder. I am more tolerant. I am more focused on them because I feel so *complete*! And I remember where it began.

The journals I kept years ago were what brought me to write here today. I remember wanting to hide them so that no one would ever find them. Whatever your secrets are, whatever your history is, when you allow them to come out on the page, you give them a chance to take off. Off the paper and into your life, the first etchings of your untold future.

On the table in your bedroom. In the bottom drawer of your desk. Take a pen to paper and start to find another life, inside the life that you have. Nothing is more fascinating than what's deep inside your mind. It's exciting in there, it's scary in there; it's painful and full of secrets. Perhaps the secret is what you long to do, in addition to what you're doing. All the feelings you have kept from yourself are waiting to be found. Every time you need a break in the day, or you feel restless and bored with your life, head north. Find out who lives up there.

Chapter 16

I walked down the hall with Melinda again. Oh, here's a familiar room. I go in here a lot. Just about every weekend and, man, is there food inside this one. We opened the door slowly, to see what mess lurked in here. Oh, my. There must have been some mistake. Someone must have already come and cleaned this one for me. There wasn't a speck of dirt, a piece of lint, not a fingerprint on the glass. The room was full of light and as perfect as a room could be. I smiled at my luck, pulled the door closed, and began my walk down the hall. "Not so fast," Melinda said. "It's not about the food." "Yes, it is," I insisted. "This room is clean, clean, clean."

Sundays at my sister-in-law's. What the heck was going on with me? What was with these Sundays? To start with, we talked about the time spent there. The reason I had such a tough time figuring it out was that I genuinely love each and every member of Scott's family. I would describe my mother-in-law as one of the finest women I know. A mentor in so many ways. My sisters-in-law are phenomenal people. And I have an added bonus; I get to be Aunt Nancy, or Aunt Weirdo, as one of them calls me. Before we had kids, those were my kids; I loved them like they were my own.

Hectic, crazy, loud, crowded, and very much not what I'd grown up with. That was somewhat tough. But it didn't explain the food bingeing. My husband would go and leave me unattended;

well, he wasn't leaving me with strangers. This was now my family, too. Conversations were fragmented, no one could speak uninterrupted, and there were kids who needed this, this, this, and that. Is that a reason to stuff your face? Everyone was so warm and loving toward me. The room was clean. It had to be the food.

These were clues without fingerprints, so I ran down the list again. A room full of people who were kinder than kind, givers not askers, and always happy to help. An extended family of aunts and uncles who were more like second parents. Nothing was too much, everyone loved them, and they were admired by all who knew them. They were a group. What a childhood they'd all had. What a perfect family they were, and how lucky I was to be with them. There it was. They were way too perfect for me.

No matter what I did, I felt I paled in comparison to them. I wanted to be one of them but I didn't feel I belonged. Apart from them I felt like a good person, giving, generous, warm, and kind. A thoughtful friend, a good daughter, a person people loved. But not selfless, not without needs, and certainly not as perfect. With them I felt so "less than." I felt like I got lost in the crowd. I didn't feel like I mattered as an individual, only as part of the group. This was all right for all of them, but I felt invisible. If I had a voice, there's no way it would be heard; the others were so much louder. Rather than feel so alone, I spent my time with the food. The entire time we were there.

The hardest part of my therapy was right here. I was able now to identify the reasons behind my eating. I could avoid certain situations that I knew were trouble. But what about the situations I knew would be trouble but I wouldn't be able to avoid? This was my frustration. As hard as I'd worked, as far as I'd come, in some ways I felt no better off. I knew why. I even understood Sundays. But I still couldn't stop the eating.

I wanted to quit. Why in the world did I have to have this? Why did I have to work so hard at something that some people, most people, didn't? Why was life so hard? It seemed so completely unfair. Why couldn't I be with my family, understand my emotions, and not stuff myself with food? The answer finally came. I hadn't made any changes. Understanding was only halfway. The food was in the next part. The part that called for my voice.

It took a long time. I had some evaluating to do, I had some choices to make, and I had some opinions that needed to be heard. I needed to learn where I should exercise my options and where I should just go with the flow. This was extremely complicated.

My sisters- and brothers-in-law were a little older than we were. They had more money than we had. Their kids were older, so they had a wisdom and experience wider and more practiced than ours. Decisions regarding the whole family were made by them. Vacations were planned, gifts were purchased, and holiday dinners were thrown. Because of the size of the family, varying circumstances, and complications, I felt we had less control. It's not that we weren't consulted and brought in on the discussions. We were. But I felt we were outnumbered by all of them, and their more complicated logistics.

My sisters-in-law are close. They're best friends, as a matter of fact. Their children are close in age, so many of their plans and philosophies are similar. It's not that we were excluded. We always had the choice to join in or sit out. My fear in not joining was that I would make Scott unhappy. My fear in not joining in was that they would be insulted or somehow take it wrong. But sometimes it wasn't the way I operated. It was theirs.

I had to assert my opinion, and that meant pushing up the volume of my choices. It meant recognizing the differences in our styles and that mine wasn't better or worse than theirs, just different. It meant making choices with Scott, putting our family first, and that bigger part of our family second. And learning that that was okay.

The first step was to cut out some of the Sundays with Scott's family and spend some of them on our own. Scott was supportive of this but he felt a pull. He wanted to be with his family. Our kids were happy there, too; after all, they got to be with their cousins. I felt very selfish in pulling us away since it worked for everyone else. So I made sure that on the Sundays we were alone, we did fun activities. In my mind I justified it in another way, too. This time together was really *together*. With Scott's family, we all disbursed.

There were more choices to exercise. On a family vacation, I could now make decisions that were right for us, not just for the larger group. I also learned that I'm more comfortable in small group settings or contact that's more one-on-one. So when the group was all together, I would seek out my nieces and nephews or one of my special aunts. I always loved connecting with them.

Emotionally, and separate from what went on with Scott's family, it meant sitting with the painful feelings I had about my not-so-happy childhood and feeling the envy of what they had as a family. That may have been the hardest part.

My sister and I never had the easy kind of relationship that my sisters-in-law have. We had terribly difficult times trying to get along, with personalities and worlds that have practically nothing in common. No, not even practically. There was nothing for us to share. Until the births of my children. Finally we shared something, and that was our love for them. And she really loves Scott, too.

Now we've found ourselves on some sort of a discovery mission and we can't seem to get enough. It's not that our lives have more in common now, because they are as different as they could be. So are our styles, outlooks, and behaviors. But, like identical twins who were reared apart, coming together in later years, we are checking out our alikeness now and we're amazed at what we see. It's not in the way we live our lives, and not in the way we think. It's in the uncanny resemblance of our responses, when some feeling or memory gets triggered. We are sisters in the truest sense; we share emotional genetics.

Now I truly look forward to our Sundays with Scott's family. I eat and enjoy whatever they have, and I'm no longer fearful of it. It's not about the food and it never was.

I had solved the issues I had with Scott's family. But in their homes was a bigger issue that I had overlooked. It was a member of his family I had never faced. Equally good, equally kind, and the one I loved most of all. Throughout my therapy, I explored every room and all the relationships except for one. I couldn't avoid it any longer. I would have to confront my marriage.

Chapter 17

There was the room at the end of the hall. It had double doors. I didn't want to open it. Scott didn't want to, either. It was so much easier to spend time in the other rooms of the house. The kids' rooms, the family room, and, certainly for me, the kitchen. It wasn't so much that we didn't want to make the room feel better. We just didn't know how to and we were much too afraid to try.

Just before Bagel Day I remember watching an old videotape from a couple of years before. I was laughing with such life and vitality. I remember wondering where that girl had gone. Where was that laugh? I felt so sad for its absence. I had no idea until much later in my therapy; my marriage was falling apart. And it had been for quite some time.

Looking back, Scott and I had ruts like anyone else. We had closer times, more distant times, but there was one time that stood apart. It was the birth of our second child and the threat we faced concerning his health. As devastating as it was at the time, it brought us very close together. It was the first time in our whole relationship that I felt like I'd gotten inside him.

Over the course of the next year, as things returned to normal and the shock of what we had gone through was settling down, I felt things move back to a very distant place. That closeness was gone and I missed it terribly. I began to eat. I began to binge. I never put it together. I was lonely for him and what we seemed to have lost. I wanted his attention. I wanted him to miss it, too. I wanted him to cuddle me, and not just when we were in bed. I had been given a taste of a wonderful feeling and I wanted to have it back.

I wanted Scott to have needs. He had none. I wanted him to have problems. He had none. I wanted him to have one bad day I could help him through. I wanted some emotion, some intimacy of thoughts that he'd share only with me. I wanted something to tell me he was there. He had needs, as it turned out. But he was too afraid to express them. He had resentments, too; he just wasn't able to say so. He came from a family that didn't do that. His way of dealing with whatever he was feeling was to retreat. He went further inside himself and further away from me.

I used to watch him while he did things, just to take him in. I loved the color of his perfect skin. I loved the back of his neck, the crinkle in the corners of his eyes, and the way tears came down when he laughed. I noticed every little detail of my husband's being. I loved him through and through. I would cry when he left for trips, which wasn't very often. I would worry about life without him. I longed for a hug from behind, a kiss on my face, or a call to say he was thinking of me. I would turn to catch him looking at me only to find that he wasn't.

Of course he loved me, he'd say. Of course he needed me. And of course he thought I was beautiful. It wasn't that he was closed off, he insisted, that was simply who he was. I wanted to go for therapy. I suggested maybe he would go, too, but he didn't feel the need. What about us? What about our distance? I knew he felt it, too. There was no intimacy in our lives, only our loving friendship. Our partnership was strong but we both knew there was so much missing. He wanted intimacy, too. He wanted a closeness and comfort that we never had. But he didn't let me know. He didn't acknowledge it ever. Not because he was wrong or uncaring; he just didn't know how to.

My hurt turned into anger. My anger turned into bitchiness. I was moody. I was temperamental. I was eating myself into misery. And then I blamed him. I blamed him for letting me eat. I begged him to sit beside me, stay with me when we went places so I wouldn't overeat. Looking back, I just wanted him to stay close. It wasn't about the food. And looking back, I can't blame him for wandering off. Who wouldn't?

I knew he had to resent me. All of my ridiculous emotional stuff. He told me he wasn't angry. He insisted there was nothing underneath. "I'm shallow," he would say, laughing. "That's who you got stuck with, shallow, boring me." I never believed him. No one could be that shallow, not even him. And he's not a boring person.

We built a life in projects. We did parties, houses, and crazy ventures that always kept us together. We were raising very happy children who loved those projects as much as we did. Doing things creatively became our family trademark. As a couple we were the very best of buddies. We did everything together. There was trust, respect, and a deep appreciation for everything we had.

There was no better husband than mine in terms of his qualities and his willingness to help in any way. He never said no, but I didn't ask for a lot material-wise; I was more demanding of his insides. He was very much there with his time and very devoted in his presence. He was the nicest person I knew and that made it all the more infuriating. I interpreted his actions as those of a nice guy. He was that nice to everyone. I didn't feel I had anything different than anybody else. As a matter of fact, I didn't.

I knew that we were in trouble. I knew we couldn't leave that room unattended and expect it to keep its condition. I told him I couldn't live like that anymore. I began to break down more and more. My therapy was bringing it all to the surface. I felt myself slipping so far from us. I was so uncomfortable living that way and I didn't want marriage if that was what marriage was. I told him I wanted out. He didn't hear me. Or maybe he really did and didn't know what to do. So he just did nothing at all.

I would stand in that room by myself. He wasn't there anymore. I looked out the window and saw someone. I felt myself longing to go there. I went back, ran down the hall, and told him what I had seen. I told him what I felt. He didn't really respond. I think he just trusted the strength of the house and the height of those open windows. Emotionally, he walked away and closed the door behind him.

Chapter 18

Melinda and I determined that I was nearing my end with her. This decision came about two years after we first started. I know what you want to know. You're not as concerned about my marriage or the choices I was making. Forget that. You want to know if I lost weight. Well, I'll give you all the numbers so I can get on with the story.

At the time I left Melinda I was about six pounds less than when I started. That was the lowest weight I had been since having my kids. I used to hit that number every so often on a diet, but only for about six and a half hours. My weight was now consistent and I was thrilled in spite of the fact that I *wasn't* my thinnest. Just so you know, that six-pound loss was still eight pounds more than what I weighed at the time we got married. Those eight pounds came off later, after I was on my own. With a three-pound fluctuation, that's where I am today. Roughly fifteen pounds less than I was. Now can I get back to my story?

This was not the first time I had thought we were done. But this was the first time Melinda did. What made it different? I was steady. Not just steady in my weight but steady in my housecleaning system. I was eating and not obsessing. I was enjoying my kids, maintaining my family and home, involving myself in various small projects, and confronting situations as they came up. I was taking acting classes once a week, which I loved. I was training for a marathon. I felt balance in my life. This place in my therapy seemed like the end of school, as the year winds down to an end.

It felt like a graduation. And since I missed out on the one from college, I decided to make this one count. It was late spring, right about the time graduations typically take place. I bought a white suit. I sent out invitations to Scott, my dad, my stepmother, Phyllis, and Melinda. The ceremony would take place in her office so it had to be very small. I didn't include my mom because I didn't know if she would have been comfortable with the way I was going about this.

Typical Melinda, always yippity-yapping about something. First it was closure with Jenny; this time it was closure with her. She would agree to whatever way I wanted to do this, unorthodox as it might be. Her concern was that in the fantasy of my exit, everyone might not perform to my expectations, and what if they didn't? What if my last session left me disappointed or uncomfortable? "Let's process this," she said. "Let's think this through. What if your father and Scott don't like me? What if you have feelings afterward and you didn't like the ending?"

She had a point. And certainly this thinking through a situation was what I had studied at University of Binge-a-Soda. I could see everyone saying things that might be uncomfortable. They may not know what to say at all. I could see Scott cracking one of his jokes and I could see me feeling icky. Melinda likely assumed I would either choose not to have them come or decide that whatever it was that they said, I would listen to it with acceptance. But no, I went for the third option. I wrote a script, made four copies, and handed them around the room. That way no one could screw it up.

Controlling? You bet. Looking back, I see where it came from. When I was growing up, my dad spent a great deal of time with us, but there wasn't an emoting bone in his body. He showed no comfort with words or affection, until much later in his life. Now he cries at every toast he makes.

Scott is very much like my dad was before he started crying at toasts. He is loving, supportive, devoted, and fun, but when it comes to emotions and words, well . . . he sucks. So I took it upon myself to make sure their words were perfect. I also wanted to have some fun. The greatest strength these two men have is their ability to laugh. Their flexible, fun personalities allowed me room to do this. And their acceptance spoke of their love.

My dad is my most glowing fan. Nothing I ever do is wrong, but he always wants me to go for more therapy. If I went every day of the week, it wouldn't be often enough. There are other opinions out there and I need to get them all. Unless of course my opinion matches his, then I'm in good mental health. Like the days I'm into my marriage and think my husband's just great; boy, am I ever together! On the days my marriage stinks and I can't stay another second, I need professional help. Never dis someone's Mini Me.

My dad, who has found out all the credentials of those whose help he has sought, in my opinion missed an important one: Melinda. My dad needs to see Melinda. Scratch that. My dad needs to be admitted full-time to Melinda. These are the calls I get from my dad:

"Nance, I've got to come for dinner 'cause I need to lose two pounds before Saturday." He always knows I won't cook anything to make him gain weight. "Nance," he says as he sucks in his gut, "do you know I haven't been at this weight since October 22, 1988? You remember, that's when I bought those yellow pants that I couldn't fit into." "Nance, I'll have to come over after tennis. I need to sweat off three more pounds." Or, "I'm going to my mother's to-night; that's a two-pound event." Or, "Nancy!"—as he puts his face in my face—"Do you think I went too far? I'm looking kind of gaunt, don't you think? I'm down to 202."

And then there is his tuxedo. As an event approaches where he'll need to wear it, there is no other topic. Not an important one any-way. It's a countdown and his discipline is impressive. I mean, it's impressive to him. I know this because he tells me how impressive that discipline is as often as he can. My beautiful, handsome, in-shape, and exceptionally athletic father is a Superball with his weight. He's way up or he's way down and he's got a whole lot of bounce back and forth.

Some of my very best traits come from my dad. I've got my dad's legs; he's got some really great-looking legs. I've got his insatiable appetite for fun; we love nothing more than to laugh. My dad is generous and warm, and he makes you feel so incredibly special whenever you're in his presence. And, last but not least, is the amount we can eat; we share an amazing capacity for food. Our stomachs can hold any amount that we load into them. He once took me out for sushi and decided he couldn't afford to again.

In my graduation-ceremony script, I mingled my dad's many words of praise for me with his total obsession with food. I had a lot of fun writing his part. He spoke of how proud he was and then asked if anyone else smelled corned beef. He thanked Melinda for all she had done and then wondered if he had eaten lunch. When everyone said he had, he asked if he had eaten breakfast.

Scott would not have known what the heck to do or say in this session. That was a truth. So I wrote him looking for a way out. I had him say how proud he was, and then reach for his beeper, as though it were going off. He would say he had an emergency call and would have to be leaving immediately. Then I had Melinda point out that he wasn't wearing a beeper. I had him talk about how much "color" I had seemed to gain in my life since beginning with Melinda. I had everyone applaud Scott at this incredible description of emotion. "No, not that kind of color," he said. "I mean she keeps painting the house different colors. I now have a purple bedroom!" I'm ashamed to admit that was true. Painting my house different colors had become one of my projects. I painted the kitchen, too. Pink. And I painted my bathroom kind of a gas-station green.

Then there was Phyllis. I once told her we needed to rename *stepmother* to "sidemother." She would have said everything right, everything warm, and all would have come straight from her heart. So I wrote in her part, and simply said that with us there was no need for scripting.

Looking back, this was an issue of trust. This was an issue of expectation and letting people fall short of that. Back then I needed them to say it right. I needed it to be perfect. Today I would have let them be who they are, and had the confidence to make it enough. Confidence coming from two places. One place is the success I feel and knowing it's mine and I own it. The second place is the trust in their love no matter how it's expressed.

Like any graduation suggests, you've completed your studies and now it's time to go off on your own. State your goals and find your course, learn more and more as you go. The classes just prepare you. They give you a base to start with. What would come in the years to follow would be nothing I could have expected. Often I wonder where I would be had I not been given that base.

As tradition states, a meal follows the graduation. I had asked my family to go on ahead so I could have some time alone with Melinda. I can't even begin to tell you what this day meant for me. It had been the hardest work I had ever done. I was just so very proud. And incredibly grateful.

Melinda had helped me turn my life around. She had rescued me. Like the helicopter that lands on the island where someone's been waiting for help, she was that first face I saw. She was the first person I talked to and she made that decision to squeeze me into her schedule when her schedule was already full. That was fateful for me. She was like an angel behind me all the way. She was strong in encouragement, loose in direction, and gentle with suggestion.

I found a mobile of hand-painted angels, so whimsical and floating. I told her I hoped she would put it somewhere that she would pass often, to be reminded of her abilities and the impact she had on my life. The only difference between those delicate, free-form ladies and Melinda is that Melinda's not quiet in flight.

She's usually late, running in frantically, and doors seem to slam behind her. She sits down so hard I swear that chair's got to break. She arranges herself, which leg goes where, takes a deep breath, and settles herself in the space. "Hi," she cheerfully says with a smile at her constant rushing. Now, that's what I call an entrance.

Melinda had handed me a card with a beautiful plant that she hoped I would plant in my yard. I knew she would miss me, too. In another setting we both know we would have been friends. I suppose there are many therapists who would have been able to help me get where I needed to go. But she was the one I found. She was the one I picked. She was the one who was there.

Cap and gown. A signed diploma. Move the tassel to the other side. I was a graduate now! I could eat and not obsess. I could maintain a healthy low weight. But had I known what the truth would eventually bring, I might have stuck with the food!

Chapter 19

I may have left Melinda's office but it wasn't without a warning. When I had finished my therapy, she suggested that Scott and I would, at some point, need to get help. For virtually our entire marriage, we lived with terrible distance and it would need to be addressed. At the time, the last thing I could think of was starting more therapy. I had worked so hard already and Scott had no interest at all. So, about six months after I left Melinda, we made a different but happy decision. We decided to have a third child.

During that pregnancy, we found out Scott's dad had cancer. The way his family dealt with it was consistent with the way they lived. They drew their strength from one another and never stopped living their lives. They cried whenever they talked about it but devoted equal time to laughter. It was never depressing to be with them; it was just very, very sad.

A few days before my father-in-law died, I put his hand on my belly. I knew it was the closest my baby would come to meeting his grandfather. I wanted so much to be there for Scott. I wanted him to need me. I wanted to be the one to help him through this, but he didn't come to me. He sought his support from his family and I felt so left out of the center. I remember crying so hard when my father-in-law died, but I felt like I cried alone.

Our distance was growing but our life was building. Scott's business was becoming more successful. We had bought a house in the country. We had our beautiful baby boy and named him after Scott's dad. Our family life, our life with our friends—outside it all came together. But inside we were apart.

My therapy was kicking in even more, now that I was on my own. Melinda had always talked about a cylinder and how it needed to be filled. I was raising three happy children. I was writing poems and invitations for people's parties, and becoming recognized for my creativity. I was decorating our country house and I was proud of what I had done. Since I had already run a marathon, my new goal was my speed. I had eaten (excuse me, that was a real typo and I couldn't resist leaving it there), *beaten* an eating disorder. I was feeling strong and accomplished.

Whenever Scott and I were drifting, the country house would bring us back. There, we would take long walks late at night. There, we broke away from routines. There, we would reconnect. And it was there I got pregnant again, about one year after our third son was born. This was completely unplanned, and I was totally shocked and upset. So was Scott. That lasted maybe two days. After that, I got very excited and I wanted the baby just as badly as if it had been planned. Scott joined me and matched that feeling. His emotions really broke through and finally I had him back. I hadn't seen that guy in six years.

I had never been happier. Never felt more in love with him. Five weeks later I miscarried and my grief was overwhelming. Scott seemed to vanish again. I hadn't just lost a pregnancy. I knew I had lost Scott again, and something inside me gave up. I could no longer wait for miracles or tragedies to be what it took to get close. That was the day, in my heart, that I walked away from my marriage.

The miscarriage and distance with Scott were followed by a series of small disasters. That fall we took on a huge project with our house and everything went wrong. You may not understand what I mean by *huge*. This project was equal in size to the lunches I used to eat. We moved our house. I mean, we picked it up off the foundation and put it somewhere else. Don't ask.

We were selling the land our house was on, but the house would have been torn down. To maximize the value of the property and the house, Scott came up with this plan. Buy a new lot, move the house onto it, then sell it again from there. Sure, honey, great idea. Do we have any Doritos?

There were complicated zoning issues. All of our neighbors gave support except for one family, and they made our lives miserable. We were renting an apartment to live in while the house got prepared to be moved, and the five of us were very cramped. The logistics of getting the kids to school and to their activities was extremely difficult. We were pretty far from our neighborhood and it was taxing on us all. We were moving from place to place since the whole thing was taking longer than planned.

Once the house was moved, the dust and mess inside were worse than I ever imagined. I felt so overwhelmed and tired. I didn't complain but I felt homesick every day. My home was unlivable and I felt like we had taken too much on. I just hated the whole thing.

Four months later we moved back into the house on the same day as a terrible snowstorm. It took us an hour just to get to the friggin' front door. Then the pipes burst, the furnace broke, and the water flooded the basement. One week later, when we were settled, something happened to me. And it scared the shit out of me.

It was Sunday. We were getting ready to take the kids to a museum. I sat down on my bedroom floor and I couldn't move. I mean that I literally could not move. The kids were running back and forth and I could see them in front of me. As though I were watching a film from the sound room, I felt like I wasn't part of the picture. And when I tried to speak I couldn't.

Scott tried talking to me. I could hear him and I knew he was worried because I wasn't responding. But I couldn't make any sound. Inside my head, I told myself, you're in some momentary breakdown. You have been through a lot and you're exhausted. Eventually, he got me to talk but I couldn't explain what had happened. We went out for the day as planned. When I came home I had the most ferocious binge, one of the worst ones I'd ever had. I just chalked it up to some very tough months. I knew that I had been a trouper and that this was just the fallout. But really, it was much more than that.

The thought of not being married forever had never crossed my mind. But this life was becoming unlivable. I felt so lonely. Everything felt so wrong. I went back to Melinda; I was in terrible trouble and I just didn't know what to do. My marriage was bringing up feelings in me that I didn't understand. I had to dive deep to find them. Living so separately from Scott emotionally was taking me back to another time. It stirred up all of the sadness of my childhood and the loneliness I had grown up with.

I've talked about connecting the food to emotions, but there is another step beyond that: connecting the emotions to childhood, and the past that sits behind feelings. I had physical and emotional responses to Scott that were frightening beyond belief. They were the exact same ones I had had as a child when I was living with my mom and Charles.

When my mom married Charles and he moved into our apartment, suddenly I was living with someone I hardly knew. There was no family relationship there, but we lived as though there was one. We would all eat dinner together with very little conversation. We never went on outings or did things all together. That would have been acceptable except for one other issue. The intimacy of living together wasn't comfortable for me without a strong connection to back it.

He was never mean or unkind. But he was very distant. Back then he was extremely formal. He was French, too, so that meant he wasn't just foreign. He *was* foreign! We all shared one bathroom. We all wiped our hands on the same towels. We shared the privacy that a family shares with none of the family comfort. We would pass one another in the hallway upstairs as though we had met once before. I was often repulsed by being around him but never understood why. Until I felt it with my own husband.

When Scott and I were first married, I felt so connected to him. I loved the smell of him, loved the look of him, and loved everything that we shared. As time went on and issues were buried, we started drifting apart. I began to develop the same feelings of discomfort around him that I had felt growing up with Charles.

Finally we went for help. We opened up our whole marriage. We went back through years of resentment and hurts we had both covered up. No matter how much we worked, they were not going away. No matter how much I didn't want to be divorced, and I can't tell you how much I didn't, there was something I didn't want more. I didn't want to go back to those feelings that I lived with as a child. I couldn't live with a stranger again.

I never would have put it together. It wasn't until I asked myself, When was the last time I felt this? I have a great name for what gets stirred up in our relationships of the present. *Leftovers*. Things that weren't finished long ago and sit behind a door. The one you open every hour for food, and feel every day in your life.

If I drank from a cup and he took a sip, I would discard the drink. If I used a towel, it had to be mine; I couldn't share one with him. Just the day-to-day normalcies of sharing a home had become so painful and disturbing. The worst part was the comparison to what I used to feel. My beautiful husband had become a man I could not bear to be around. I was uncomfortable in my own home.

Imagine your family is aboard the *Titanic*. Your kids are sound asleep. You just got word that in only four hours the ship will be underwater. You look at their little faces. They're so peaceful, cozy, and warm. Yet you know what's going to happen and it's only a matter of time. That's exactly what it felt like. We knew we had to separate and would probably get divorced. This ship we were on, carrying our kids, was eventually going to sink. And there was nothing we could do to save it.

Sitting with the realization was horrifying. It was impossible. It just didn't make sense at all. And yet it was where we were. We had been in therapy, we had come to decisions, and this was not on impulse. Unfortunately it felt all too right.

That day came with a lot of preparation. I had my dad take our younger son out for the morning. We would be explaining this to him later, in a way he could understand it. We called the two older kids into our room for a family "powwow." At the time they were nine and eleven years old. I asked my son to bring in five quarters and put them in a bowl. We all sat down on the floor and I started my demonstration. This was surreal. This was preparing them for the sinking ship and putting their life jackets on. I needed to be calm and let them know we would all get through this together. Somehow I was on autopilot, one of those strong parental moments. Scott stayed very quiet, but strong in support for the kids.

"These five quarters represent our family," I said. "Do you

know why? Because they are strong, shiny, and unbreakable. Can you break these quarters in half?" They put the quarters in their hands and agreed that they couldn't. I put the quarters back in the bowl and then I removed one of them. "This quarter is one of you at camp. Does that mean we're not family?" They all shook their heads no. I put it back into the bowl. "This quarter is Daddy and he's at work. Does that mean we're not family?" No. "So that means that being apart at times does not change the way we feel, right?" They nodded.

Then I took out two of the quarters and put them next to each other. I put the other three quarters below them. "These two quarters are Daddy and me; these three below are you guys. The love that parents have for their children never ever changes. It only gets bigger every day, no matter what you do. Sometimes, though, the love that a husband and wife have for each other can change. Daddy and I love each other very much, but there is a certain kind of love that a husband and wife should have for each other. We don't have that, and we need some time to understand why. The best way for us to do that right now is to spend some time apart. But we are still a family and we will always be your parents. That can never change." I went on to explain exactly what this meant.

Our priority was to keep the kids in their home every night. We didn't want to disrupt them any more than we had to. We rented an apartment so that we could alternate nights out while the other stayed in the house. I explained to the kids exactly how this would work. I answered all of their questions. I remembered my own parents' words more than thirty years before. I knew what had been missing. I knew how to make them feel safe.

"Daddy and I have a promise to make to you. We promise that you will grow up in a happy home. If our being married would make us so unhappy that we couldn't keep that promise to you, then we would not be able to stay married. No matter what happens, and we don't have that answer yet, you guys will grow up happy and be very well taken care of by both of us. That doesn't mean we won't have sad days. People can have sad things happen, but it doesn't mean they're not happy people."

I told them that we all felt sad in this moment and that we all needed to feel that. I told them we would be checking in on their feelings about this on a daily basis. I told them they would see us doing the same for each other. After we talked and answered their questions I told them we would all get showered and dressed. We had planned some fun outings for the day. I would take my daughter shopping and Scott would take the boys to a museum.

Our kids were amazing. The initial shock and sadness moved to curiosity about what would happen. During the course of the day we talked about it a lot as we kept active with what we were doing. They asked if we would date. I answered them honestly that eventually we would. They asked if we would get divorced. I told them it was possible but not something we could answer today. They asked if there might be another house. I answered them that if that happened it would be gradual, something we would all figure out together. They asked if they would get a bigger room and what they could buy to go in it. I just laughed in amazement at them.

They never seemed fearful. We hovered over them with a lot of talking, but kept laughter and life going strong. Their behavior never changed and we looked for that everywhere. We talked to their teachers, put out alerts, but there was simply nothing to see. I think they trusted the solidity we showed them. Over the course of the next few weeks we were so focused on them, and they liked the attention they got. The kids were fine. I mean, they didn't even get wet. It was the rest of the world that wasn't.

We had sent a shock wave through our family, friends, and acquaintances the likes of which we had never expected. They weren't just sad. They were deeply affected and wounded. How could this happen to Nancy and Scott? Didn't they have the perfect marriage? I think it scared them. If this could happen to the *Titanic,* the strongest ship ever built, what did that say for the others?

During that time apart we each became stronger and more confident. We also saw the strength in our need to look out for each other. There was not ever a dispute about money. If anything, we were each worried about the other. We each went out on some dates. We called each other on the way and told each other about them. I made sure dinner was waiting for him if it was his night to be in the house. He continued to be protective of me and we both spent a lot of time with the kids.

I suppose it sounds strange. It was. But in a funny way it was us.

We had always had a very deep friendship and a need to look out for each other. What was wrong with us was very wrong, but what was right was very right. Honestly, being separated felt similar to being married. We took care of each other in the same way. We just didn't live together.

I remember noticing that food wasn't an issue at all. The sadness, the fear, the total disbelief, was never played out in my eating. I remember lying in bed, one of my nights in the apartment, staring at the ceiling and trying to imagine how life had brought me here. But food was never a problem. I knew why. This separation was true and right. Pain doesn't cause me to overeat. Living against the truth always does.

How did we come back together? Bruce Willis again. I was out to dinner with my girlfriends about two months into our separation. I was talking about the way that Scott and I were taking care of each other. One of the women, who didn't even know me that well, told me I *had* to rent the movie *The Story of Us,* about a couple divorcing. I rented it that night. I sobbed at the end as they came back together with their flashbacks of history and family. I called Scott the very next day and described the movie to him. I told him we had so much, and the movie had made me see it. We came back in a rush and a flurry.

What really happened after the Hollywood ending? We would sink many times again. But somehow we've never bailed. Maybe it is us. Maybe it is for the kids. I guess it is some of both.

Walking into the room with the big double doors, you would see little that looks the same. We are different people. We have a different marriage. We have a caring and respect for each other that is solid, lasting, and strong. We have an honesty that would blow you away. We are not afraid of our words. We are not afraid of our thoughts. We laugh at all of our nightmares and I cry for some of those dreams. Are we forever? Who knows, but we're certainly for today. The time apart taught us something very important. If we ever choose to bail, we know where the life jackets are. If we never choose to bail, then this is one heck of a ship.

Whatever brought us here was necessary; I would never trade in what we've learned. Have the issues changed? Not really. What changed is the way we look at them and the choices we make around them. Is it better or is it worse? Yes. It's better and it's worse. Better because it's honest, worse because it hurts, and freeing to stop living falsely.

I had gotten a warning from Melinda and ignored it. That's why yours comes in bold print:

Food obsessions kill marriages. They distract us from the real problems. They make us believe that our problems with food are the only ones worth solving. They give us an excuse. They distance us from our spouses. They make us unapproachable and they take up all of our focus. Certainly it's the problems in marriage that can trigger their existence. Or the marriage is fine but our other issues can keep us away from closeness. So we develop an intimate relationship with food and keep everyone else away.

Do you overeat around your spouse? Do you avoid going out to dinner because you don't want to deal with the food? Do you go to bed before your spouse to keep yourself from eating? Is it really the food you're avoiding? Think. Are you staying up in the kitchen eating while your spouse has gone to bed? What if you were alone? Would you still be up eating, instead of going to bed? What are you really avoiding when you go to bed separately?

What you don't want to deal with is all that discomfort that is present in your marriage. The reason the food is all you can see is because you fear you can't handle the truth. As you read these pages I know what you're thinking. "Oh, no, we're very happy. For me the problem is food." That is what I said, too. "I'm in love with my husband, we have a great marriage, and my problem is just with the food." Uh-huh.

All of that having been said, maybe this is the best time to give you the name of the diet that made me finally lose weight. The one that kept it off for good, leaving me the body I always dreamed of. The diet is called The Truth. Maintenance requires facing those feelings every single day.

When you follow the Truth diet, it may take you places you never imagined, much like it did in my marriage. Food keeps it all in a pattern, so you always know what comes next. Diet, lose weight, diet, lose weight; at least that's as bad as it gets. *Groundhog Day.* Did you see that movie? Every morning, the main character's alarm clock goes off, and the guy keeps waking up to the exact same day, over and over again. Finally, he learns what he has to do to wake up to a different day.

Brrrrriiiiiiiiiiiiing. The alarm clock just went off. Which day is it for you?

Chapter 20

I had to hide it or you wouldn't have waited. I had to bury it in an unnamed chapter or you would have skipped the rest and raced to this one. But you forget how well I know you, and know the way you think. You sneak past the pages and approach that one: the one that talks about food. I'm silently waiting behind the page. I wait without taking a breath. My heart is pounding in anticipation like a predator waiting for prey. Here you come, your fingers go to the corner, and you quietly turn the page. BOO!

I want to spy on your denial. I think you're relating to a lot of my emotions and finding my stories compelling. But you're separating yourself, aren't you? Because your stories are different you somehow believe that this is not about you. And what worked for me will not work for you; what we have is entirely different.

This is one of those moments when knowing your name would help. Hey, you! You couldn't be more wrong. It is you. It doesn't matter if you are different than I am. Your personality, lifestyle, and economic situation needn't be the same as mine. Your weight can be far above mine, or far below. I don't care what your story is. If you're obsessing about food, you belong here.

In my old school of food, I used to learn about calories. I used to study diets. I was graded on a scale (Oh, shit, that one was good).

Now I'm in graduate school, which is where I study emotions. I never feel caught up since the subjects change so often. Food mimics life, so the patterns are just the same.

It's time to talk about food. If the convict got in for stealing money, he might have learned that stealing is wrong, but what happens when the job he's offered is at a bank? If we know that when our emotions are whacky food gets out of hand, what are we supposed to do when there's food everywhere we go? What about "normal" eating? Do we even know what that is? Would it be possible that *food* and *normal* could be written in the same sentence?

Just a couple of things I need to say as we move into phase two with food. We need to be light. We need to laugh. We need to remember that although eating obsessions are our own personal nightmare, they are simply unattended feelings that feel worse because they're unattended. We need to keep it in perspective. Even when we can't.

Just because you feel like you're dying doesn't make it so. It just feels that way right now. Feeling depressed, lonely, lifeless, hopeless, and wanting just to give up? Great, now we have something in common! Feel like life will never be better and your future could be even worse? Okay, just let me ask you one question. What is up with that hair? C'mon, honey, lighten up. Your sense of humor is what you'll need to keep from sinking too deep in your pain.

There was a day I believed I would never be able to eat "normally" and without fear. But standing in my kitchen today with my two boys, Sam and Alex, my daughter, Lani, and her adorable friend Samantha, I actually ate *two* bologna sandwiches. Not just the crusts off theirs. Why? Because I was hungry and that's what I wanted.

Of course, I don't typically have two sandwiches. That lunch was bigger than usual. But guess what? It stopped right there. Will I skip dinner? Never. I'll eat again tonight. My dinner will be smaller than usual but one of my choice. I'll consider the lunch I ate and make a choice that's reasonable. That is not an eating disorder; that is weight management. But I had to swim through the eating disorder in order to live in the sandbar.

Think of the next chapters as my house, and I have invited you over. I'll tell you right now you won't be leaving early! I won't let you go until everything's been covered. We'll talk about the journals and how important they are for keeping food and emotions in check. We'll talk a lot about food. We'll shop for it, cook it, and learn how to structure it. Whether you believe it or not, what you eat is not the problem. *How* you eat is crucial to weight loss. When a diet works it's because of the structure. When it fails it's because of restriction. You will learn to structure foods that you like, and enjoy the diet of your cravings.

We'll look over restaurant and fast-food options, since we no longer need to avoid them. You'll learn to eat but not *overeat*. We'll discuss snacks, meal planning, and we'll even walk through a binge. Sometimes they happen, you know, so we'll learn how to lighten the load. We'll even talk about the day *after* a binge and the best way to get back on track. You'll learn how to make everything feel safe. And yes, this is how you'll lose weight.

We're going to discuss choices that come from three places. One place is in food, and you will choose from all the foods that you like. You'll learn to balance mostly healthy foods with junky foods if you want them. When you allow yourself the choice, there is no need to abuse the privilege. Another place is learning to make decisions from the strong part of who you are, and what you know about yourself, since much of our overeating has to do with making choices against what we really feel. And last, you'll need to choose goals in your life that aren't just about your weight. Water doesn't boil when you watch it, right? It boils when you step away. The same is true of your weight. Life begins after food. Stick around and I'll prove it.

So far, we've learned to Separate Always Food and Emotions with SAFE, and that helps us with our food issues. But SAFE Part Two is about living beyond food. What does SAFE stand for here? Separate Always *Feelings* and *Events*! Is it the situation you can't live with? Or is the situation, just like the food, covering something else? Ah-so! *Sí, señora. Avez-vous une ISSUE? Oui, oui, madame! MUCHO GRANDE* ISSUES. *Oy gavolt*, have I got some issues for you! You'll be hearing all about those.

Hey, this is all about us. And isn't that our favorite topic? That and food, of course. I've got a great idea. We'll have our own slumber party. I'll lend you my flannel pants and I'll grab a T-shirt for you. We'll raid the fridge, cozy up on our pillows, and stay up all night talking. So go put on your jammies. We're in for one very long night!

Chapter 21

*L*et's get started with the biggest food problem of them all: how to stop your bingeing. The answer comes in sections. This chapter will focus on both preventing and preparing for binges and downsizing them as they occur. Later, after we've had some lunch, we'll learn how to walk through a biggie. We wouldn't want to talk about bingeing when we're hungry, right?

You have been advised by every specialist on the subject of emotional eating. They suggest you express yourself, distract yourself, engage yourself, satisfy yourself, and relieve your need for that binge. Nothing works, right? It didn't work for me either.

I remember reading a good book called *Overcoming Overeating*. It suggested that if we allow ourselves all the foods we are deprived of, we won't be compelled to overindulge; that it's the deprivation of them that makes the eating so crazed. I rushed to the store and filled my cart with every food I had ever wanted. Now this was my kind of shopping!

The concept is right and true. I live by that today, but I wasn't ready to live by it then. On a day that was emotionally uneventful, the food being around was okay. Unfortunately, though, when binges would unexpectedly happen and I wasn't yet savvy in understanding or avoiding them, it only made it worse to have that food so close. I had to get rid of it. It was too dangerous for me given where I was at the time.

Here are some other pearls of wisdom that infuriate me. They tell us to put the food where we can't see it. Duh. Make the food hard to get to. Oh, please. Any respectable binger knows how to climb onto a counter. Or run out to 7-Eleven. Don't eat for stress or loneliness and don't eat for comfort, they say. Don't fill voids with food. Call a friend, they suggest. Do something active, like take a walk or a bike ride. Pick up a book, write a letter, or start a household project. Get out of the house, go work out, make yourself busy with goals. Yeah, right.

I don't know anyone in the throws of an obsession who can just simply put it away to go sew a pair of pants. If it were that easy, we wouldn't be listening to all of the experts! Telling us it's emotional eating and telling us not to eat for that reason is like telling us not to cry because crying never solves anything. Now tell me where to put my tears.

As the food was pushed past my lips, as my hands trembled with each food I unwrapped and opened, silly me didn't think to put it down and go to Europe. Call a friend? Sorry, it just doesn't work that way. No one calls a friend from a binge. It's private, it's frenzied, and it's way past the point of help.

All that matters in that moment is the food. No one and nothing can stop it. The walk around the block ain't gonna cut it. Not when there's a cinnamon-pecan coffee cake right at your shaking fingertips. I used to put cakes and cookies in the freezer, thinking that would make them unavailable. Guess what I learned? I like them better frozen.

Hiding food won't work either. Every year around the holidays, my father-in-law's company used to send big, fat almond-chocolate bars. I had Scott hide the box so I wouldn't eat them, and then I spent half the day searching for them. I hunted them down like a bloodhound. There's a song that describes our commitment to finding food when we need it. "Climb every mountain, ford every stream, / Follow every rainbow, till you find ice cream." Now, let the rat have the floor.

Here's how to preempt a binge. Let's say you just finished lunch with a friend. As you get in your car to head home, suddenly you feel that rumbling of nervous energy. You suddenly think about food. You know that the second you walk through your door, you'll immediately go to the kitchen and eat. This is your pivotal moment.

Something just happened or is about to happen. Go back over the lunch or think about what awaits you at home. Sit in the car and feel it. What is it? Think some more. When did you start to get anxious? Don't walk into your house until you give yourself some time here. Don't think about the food. Force yourself to face what you're feeling.

Here's a real-life, Nancy example. Scott took the boys to visit his cousins in Wisconsin for the weekend and my daughter and I stayed back at our house in the country. It was nice and quiet, just the two of us. Saturday we did a whole day of pampering girlie stuff and Sunday we were just going to relax. The morning was going so well, even the guy who details my car came by to see if I wanted it detailed. I hadn't seen him in a year. And what is the likelihood that he would come by the very next day after my dog threw up in my car?

He left with my car and that's the last memory I have of the day as it was supposed to go. The phone rang. He told me he was on the side of the road and my car had just died on him. Apparently it had no oil. I mean *no oil*. His guess was that my two-year-old engine had "seized." Apparently this is not a good word for engines.

So, I took my neighbor's car to meet him where he was. My roadside service informed me there was no one to pick it up. Car glitches ain't my area. And of course Mr. Get-me-out-of-car-glitches was in friggin' Wisconsin. With lots of his own oil. So my detail guy called a buddy of his to tow my car to the dealer. The closed-on-Sunday dealer.

My daughter was on her computer. She was not interested in taking a bike ride or doing anything with me. It was hot out and very, very quiet. It sounds like my idea of the perfect day, stuck in my beautiful surroundings with nowhere to go. But somehow I found myself slumpy, frumpy, depressed, and tired. I knew what it was. I was in a bad place with Scott and was feeling depressed about that. I crawled into bed and dozed off.

Forging out of bed thirty minutes later, I knew the only thing that sounded worthwhile was to go into the kitchen and eat. I knew I was bored, frustrated, and down. Years ago, I would have just gone to the food. But here's what I did instead. I let myself feel bad. I complained to myself for a while. And then you know what I did? I decided I'd had enough and I needed to stop engaging in the feelings (like I used to engage in the food) and make my daughter take a bike ride with me.

This is it in a nutshell. Had I tried getting away from the food or the feeling *without* feeling it, since it was most certainly there, I may have successfully done it for a time. But I would have binged sometime later. When does a child stop nagging? As soon as that child's been heard. Hear yourself. It's the only way to get past the feeling.

While we're learning to do what Melinda called "sitting with the feelings" sometimes we'll be successful and sometimes we'll fumble. When we fumble we need the food. I know that is bad news, but it's your familiar means of coping and it won't go away overnight. But it will diminish gradually.

That "food switch" is not a food switch. It's a feeling switch. Sitting with the feelings means feeling those ants in your pants. It is so uncomfortable and so ridiculously hard that you just can't take it anymore. Whatever the present feeling is, it makes you crazy inside. The eating becomes a way to spend energy and to take you away from the feeling.

Sometimes it will be a depression like the one I felt that afternoon. It has nothing to do with *what* you're depressed about; we all get depressed sometimes. What matters is what you do with it and your ability to let yourself feel it. I don't argue with depression. I feel it. I don't try to talk myself out of it or think I shouldn't have it. If I have it, I have it. Talking myself out of it only makes me more depressed and often leads me to eat.

I wonder if I can draw a parallel here and if you're ready to see it. Let's give it a go. You know how you talk yourself out of food? You believe you're not entitled to have it and if you do it will make you gain weight? Translate that to life. You're talking yourself out of feelings, thinking you don't have the right to feel them. Why? Because we have conditioned ourselves to believe that feeling depressed is abnormal. It's not something that healthy people do. Especially when they have such nice lives and there are so many people who don't.

Am I not entitled to feel depressed about issues in my marriage just because I have a nice husband? And because there are some people who wish for what I have? Why wouldn't I allow my own feelings, no matter what they are? No matter what anyone else would think or feel if they were in my shoes? Do I need to answer to them?

Whenever we feel something really bad, we try really hard not to feel it. As though indulging ourselves in a feeling, like indulging ourselves in food, means that we are weak, ungrateful, and pitiful people. No willpower with food. No ability to be happy. Poor pathetic us.

I don't think that feeling depression is necessarily something to cover. I'm not talking severe depression that doesn't let up. I'm talking about the up-and-down, every-other-minute kind that feels severe in the moment. The kind that comes up in emotional people with every fourth breath that we take. I believe it's as natural as happiness, and I don't try to get rid of that!

Feeling bad feels bad. So, what's so bad about that? When the switch goes on just feel it. Let yourself feel awful. It isn't weak to feel shitty. It takes a strong person to feel awful and admit that they're not always happy. There is life after awful. There are happy moments to follow over and over again.

The bag of my feelings is loaded up with every extreme there is. For a deep-feeling, emotional, sometimes volatile, and sensitive creature like myself, all it takes sometimes is one small nothing and, *whoops,* there goes another feeling that just popped out of the bag. I can't help it. It's like a burp I didn't know was coming. So all I can say is excuse me.

The first way to preempt that binge is to feel. The second way to make that binge go away is to eat. Sorry, but it's a fact. There will be those times you won't get to the emotion or underlying cause fast enough or you won't be able to stick with it long enough. And you'll find yourself entering a binge. If you need to, and at times you will, just accept it. Once I let myself have that binge, telling myself it was okay, I got through it faster, with less food, and moved on to that bike ride or outing. But I needed to get through the binge first.

Distraction from the feeling will postpone it temporarily, but it will rear its ugly head again later. Guaranteed. By letting yourself have the binge, but in a more controlled and planned-for manner, you're allowing it if it's necessary. Fighting it only makes it stronger. Don't fight it. Negotiate.

What I will do now is help you plan for the binge, be prepared for the binge, not be afraid of the binge, and let it run its course. I am going to help you say yes to the very thing you've been fighting. I know that sounds outrageous to you, but for me, accepting it was the first step in controlling it. One day, when you live past the food, you'll be accepting something else you've been fighting. But for now, let's accept the food.

I know you don't believe that you can afford to be okay with any eating, especially a binge. So let me ask you some questions. Has not accepting it made it any better? Has fighting it worked to make those binges smaller and less frequent? Has anything worked?

This is where I'll ask that you trust me. If you allow it, the binges will become smaller and smaller, and probably right away. You won't gain weight; you'll lose weight because the binge will be smaller. And it's the binges that cause the weight gain. You hear me? It's overeating that causes weight gain. Eating does not make you fat and it never will. Not when it comes from your hunger. Eating junk does not make you fat either. Ridiculous quantities do.

We need to make your surroundings feel safe. You will have to figure out which foods feel safe to have and which foods you consider a threat. For now, if you live with other people, ask them to be patient with you for a while. It won't hurt them not to have huge quantities of those foods around. As far as the outside world and all of that food, we'll deal with that a bit later. For now let's safeguard the home.

You need to stock your kitchen with good, healthy, and satisfying foods. Not diet foods but foods that represent a range of choices. You need healthy foods, along with foods you'll regard as treats and desserts. Whatever makes you comfortable is what you'll have in your kitchen. If that means only low-fat, low-calorie foods, so be it. If healthy, low-fat food makes you feel like there's nothing worth eating, then you need to find what you do like. This is not a diet. It's also not a force-feeding. You need to keep what feels safe to you.

Odd as it may seem, I want you to have some sort of binge-stock, food to eat when you're in trouble. You need to make sure that there is something around in case you need it, but try to keep the choices a little less severe. For instance, if ice cream is something you binge on, make sure you buy fat-free frozen yogurt or ice cream lower in fat. Don't buy a gallon; buy a pint. Don't buy two pints; buy one.

If it's crunchy snacks you seek, buy some lower-fat versions of what you like. Instead of Pringles, Doritos, and Cheetos, try flavored rice cakes, low-fat chips, or pretzels. Buy small bags, not those super sizes, right? If you want the Doritos, that's fine. Buy them in lunch-sized bags. We are stocking up on artillery that we will be using on ourselves. Buy cap guns, not magnums. Enough for a small-town showdown, not the Civil War.

You are choosing to have foods available in the event that you'll need them. You are building your best defense against your weaker moments. You're cutting yourself some low-fat slack.

Chapter 22

You hear that pounding and scratching? That's me trying to break down the door. I need you to be open to the idea that diets and plans don't work, unless it's a plan that you've made. I need you to see that following any rule with food is the best way to put on weight, unless the rules are your own. C'mon, my manicure is chipping! How about a compromise? Just open the door a crack and I'll tell you what's coming up.

We're going to talk about diets that call themselves "diets," and diets that call themselves "This is not a diet, this is a way of life." No matter what they call themselves, if they suggest you stay away from certain foods, that is restrictive, and *that leads to overeating!*

We're going to talk about breakfast, lunch, dinner, and snacks. We'll go to the grocery store. We'll go to restaurants and look at the menu. Exercise needs to be covered and we'll need to talk about goals. We'll sit in the middle of many small moments where food is out of control, and we'll walk through those moments together. I have some stories I want to tell you, some stuff you might relate to. For starters, though, let's talk about those diets and plans.

If you are someone who diets most or all of the time except when you "cheat," overeat, or binge, then I imagine you'll feel safest with the foods on your particular plan. Whatever you're doing, I'll ask you to *try* to compromise on your rigidity. Sounds too scary? Let's ease your fear with some logic.

I'll tell you what; you do the math. Add the calories of one week's worth of cheats or binges. For example, if it's 2,800 total calories a week you think you're investing in picks, overeating, or binges, then divide that number in half. That comes to 1,400 calories. Let's take those 1,400 calories and divide them by 7, the number of days in a week. We're going to add those 200 calories back into each day of your week. Out of the 2,800 calories from overeating, you have given yourself two gifts. One is the additional calories put back into your day without it being a cheat. The second is the 1,400 calories you're saving, which goes to weight loss. And that's if you binge like a bird.

However, if you binge like the carnivorous beast that I was, your binges in a whole week could add up to anywhere between, oh, my gosh, in the many, many thousands of calories. I know that I could have easily added a minimum of five hundred calories a day and still been ahead of the game.

What a shame my math classes didn't have story problems with calories. I never would have flunked them. The point is that bingeing and overeating packs on a ton of calories and fat. Common sense will tell you that your weight gain comes from there. So we need to get you to add some calories back into your days with those exact foods that you never allow. Imagine not needing to cheat, since you get the food anyway.

Let's talk about a protein diet followed strictly. In simple terms, it requires eating very few carbs, little to no fruit, and no sugar. The good news? There is practically no restriction of protein, vegetables, or fats. Everyone is excited because they get to eat virtually unlimited quantities of rich, fattening foods. After previous and failed attempts with low-fat diets that offered boring foods in small portions, this is a piece of cake. Oh, sorry, I know you can't have cake on a protein diet since carbs and sugar are the enemy. Protein is your bread and butter. Oh, geez, sorry again. That was an insensitive slip of the tongue. Well, that's the way the cookie crumbles. *Whoa* there. Hey, sometimes you need to be harsh in order to make a point.

Guess what I see as I watch my friends on the Atkins diet. I see them cutting out their carbs and loving that unlimited meat. I see them losing weight. I see them reading labels and making decisions by the numbers of "carb grams" they see. Then, as they stay on the diet longer, I see them picking at the carbs in small bites, small tastes, and small cheats. Often they gain the weight back. Why? Because they long for carbs and they get tired of depriving themselves. The excitement of bacon, peanut butter, and bunless cheeseburgers can get old after a while. They crave a meal of fruit. They long for a piece of bread. Or they long for the entire loaf.

I'm sure for many, the Atkins plan is wonderful. It has helped so many people lose weight with foods that satisfy them. However, keep in mind that the Atkins plan deals specifically with food. It doesn't deal with emotions, deprivation, or the moments of craving those carbs. The restriction of carbs invites overeating and bingeing down the line.

And I have one other concern. High amounts of protein can have a negative affect on our health. This comes from many studies that link protein as a cause of or contributor to some diseases and conditions. Many people eat the protein and fats but bypass the vegetables. Their focus is on losing weight and not on their overall health. These are your personal decisions. This is information for you to gather on your own. I made my own decisions about what works best for *me*. You'll need to do the same.

I love carbs. I eat them every day, though I try to balance them with protein. I love meat and peanut butter, too. If I feel like having bread, I don't want filet mignon. If I feel like having a cookie, a burger ain't gonna cut it. If I want a refreshing bowl of fruit, I don't think I'll find fish refreshing. Why shouldn't I have what I want? Because if I have it, I can't lose weight? Bullshit!

Remember, aside from the emotional causes of bingeing, a huge component of your overeating is from undereating and simply wanting food. Here's a question for those of you on protein diets. When you cheat and overeat, is it with protein? Of course not. When you cheat, it's on the carbs you love. You pick and cheat on the foods you want and usually that food exceeds hunger. Then you return to the diet and the pattern repeats again. That's one tough way to keep weight off.

For the same calories as the nonstop eating and picks I used to have, here's what I could have added to each day. A warm roll or two pieces of bread on a big turkey sandwich. A nice piece of chocolate cake following a healthy salad. A small bag of potato chips as a snack. A cheeseburger on a bun for dinner would have been fewer calories than picking off of my kids' plates after having my own sorry-ass meal that didn't satisfy me. I could have had all of the foods in my binges in smaller quantity. And been consuming far less food overall.

Again, all of that overeating spread out over the week but cut in half would in fact be considered a diet. Half of a binge? That's a whole lot of food. A lot to eat freely without guilt. A lot to cut out to lose weight. Once you give up that enormous quantity, the quantity that is necessary only because you tell yourself you can't have what you want, you begin to lose weight. It makes sense, doesn't it?

What if you are not bingeing or dieting? You may be someone who eats what you want when you want it, and you don't even care anymore. You hate "diet food," the thought of anything with rules makes you crazy, and you have accepted that this is the body you have. You have given up hope of being thinner. Here's what I will tell you. If you are happy with your physical and emotional self, you're high on energy and feeling healthy, all the power to you. But if you're not, let me tell you what I think. I think you've given up, all right, but it has nothing to do with your weight. I think you've given up on yourself.

If you rebel against diets, I'm with you on that. But if you rebel against structuring food, think again. Is it the structure and the social importance placed upon being thin that you rebel against, or is it something else in your life? Who are you angry at? A diet? A society that tells you to be thin? Why would you be angry at that if it truly means nothing to you? Your decision not to go on a diet can be a sound and healthy one. It needn't come from an angry place.

Perhaps what you're rebelling against is something that hurts. Someone or something that happened. Do you get angry when nose piercing becomes the thing to do, or do you just decide it's not for you? Do you rebel when a clothing store opens and the clothes they sell look stupid, or do you simply decide not to shop there? Remember, food is food. It is not comfort, it is not anger, and there is nothing to give up on. It is also not rebellion. Your rebellion is about something else. Don't confuse it with food and make your body and health pay the price. Deal with the real source underneath that rebellious side of your eating.

On the flip side, I once heard a quote from a very skinny celebrity who said she liked being thin because it made people mad. Why does she want to make them mad? What is behind her statement? And why do people get mad at her if she is not a part of their lives? Really! Perhaps people use their weight like a ball and need to throw it in somebody's face. But whose face is it really aimed at?

Think of getting closer to that other body that lives inside you. The one that is a bit smaller. Or the one that is a bit larger. The one that reflects who you are, and not who you are fighting.

Repeat these words after me: "I am not going to diet." You will tap into better health and a general feeling of energy and strength. You will make balanced choices with food because you are capable of that. If you listen to your body, it will give answers in the way it feels. It will feel better from healthy food. It may ask for junk sometimes. It will tell you when you have eaten too much, in the form of not feeling well. Your natural cravings, when allowed, guide you to foods you want and need, and emotions that need your attention.

I know you may be concerned about portion control. Don't worry about that; you will always have enough. If you want more you'll have more, providing that you're hungry. You'll stay away from larger quantities, not because of your weight but because you just feel better when you eat that way. Again, it will be your choice to have it and your choice to pass it up. No obsession, no guilt, no fear, and no remorse.

If you hardly eat all day, we need to change that, too. You need to eat meals and you'd be foolish to ever skip them. I never, ever skip a meal; it only makes me overeat later. I learned that even if I don't think I am hungry, if it's been several hours, I am better off to eat. If I ate breakfast in the morning, I don't wait much longer than noon to eat lunch. I found that if I waited much longer than that, once I sat down to eat I ended up overeating, not having realized how hungry I was. Let me clarify that point.

We are learning to eat from hunger, that's true. We want to get out of the habit of eating when we're not hungry. If it is noon and we're not hungry, we can wait an hour or so. But adding hours beyond that is asking for trouble. I would rather err on the side of caution. Put it this way. If I eat a meal when I'm not terribly hungry, but knowing that I haven't eaten in several hours, that's a lot fewer calories than I would eat later on when I'm starved. Eating when you're starving is a dangerous time to eat.

You will make your own decisions, and if you don't like something, you won't eat it. Try to show some flexibility in trying new things, some healthier alternatives that you just might like. Again, you can lose weight no matter what you like to eat. But you will feel better if it's achieved in a healthy manner. And it will make the total difference in how you look and live. By the way, skipping meals won't make you lose weight faster. Don't think about how long it will take, just focus on today. The weight will come off naturally.

I have always had an interest and desire to be thin and in good physical shape. But I have an equally strong desire to be healthy. I don't want to be sick. I don't want to be weak. I want to keep my youth for as long as I possibly can.

Exercise is a part of this, too, and we'll talk more about that later. Do I love working out? Sometimes I really don't. Sometimes I am *so* not in the mood. But I assure you that every time I do it, it awakens me. It taps into my core. It confirms in me that I have it. I can pull myself out of a mood, a slump, or a low point. It invigorates me, gives me an escape, and it reminds me that I didn't take the easy way out. I got myself out and I did it. Every single time I work out, especially on the days I don't want to, I say these words out loud when I've finished: "Good girl! You're the best!" And I repeat it over and over. Nothing feels better than "I did it."

In anything you do, whether it's a lesson you've taught your kids, succeeding in work, finding the best prices, serving a homemade meal, or planting your very own garden, there's the satisfaction of knowing your part in the celebrated outcome. There's nothing like the feeling when you stand back and see the results of your efforts and work.

You could have had the meal delivered, but you didn't; you put it all together yourself. You could have been handed money or won it in a bet, but you worked hard and you got there instead. Landscapers didn't put those flowers in the ground; you did. And you look at them every day.

When I look in the mirror, I don't just see my small size. I see that I never gave up. I feel the accomplishment of the emotional and physical work it took to get here. That's why I take care of myself. It's why I eat mostly healthy foods and it's why I make the commitment to exercise. I have made an investment in myself; I'm very protective of my portfolio. I want to show you what else I protect.

Chapter 23

The Kitchen. If you're anything like I was, the kitchen felt about as safe as Central Park at four o'clock in the morning. And you're sitting on a bench with ten thousand in cash. And your T-shirt says "Beat me up and take my money." And all the cops are on strike. Okay, you get the point.

If your kitchen is a place of fear and anxiety, you need to make it safe. You need to make it clean. Sounds stupid? It's not stupid, it's key. You cannot have a kitchen that matches frenzied emotions. Your kitchen must appear calm, clean, inviting, and attended. If the kitchen is where you turn to when you're in trouble, let it look professional. Will it stop a binge? No. But organization and cleanliness breed control. Your kitchen needs to be clean and it's a top priority, trust me.

You need to clean out the cabinets (you can even wipe them down) and throw out foods that are old or that no one eats. If you see foods that are threatening, get rid of them. You're making the kitchen safe, but you don't want to make it sparse. That's why it's important to clean it out; so you can bring in the fresh and new.

I pull everything out and put it back like second-graders lined up for the school assembly, every item in size order. Hey, I never said I wasn't compulsive, but sometimes it comes in handy. I make my cabinets neat and efficient-looking. My refrigerator is clean and not full of foods and condiments that no one ever uses. We all know how many times we open those doors each day. Make it pleasing to look at, not cluttered and unappetizing. I like bowls of fruit and nice clean shelves. I put leftovers in Rubbermaid because it looks more organized than individually wrapped odds and ends.

I have one cabinet that holds the you-know-what food. I'd hate to have to waste steps going back and forth for a binge! I keep it stocked, as you know, but I keep it clean as well. I throw out things that are old and stale; on a bad day I might inhale them.

You have your notebooks, right? One for food monitoring and one for journaling feelings. That's the book where you can talk to yourself, you can talk to me, or you can talk to someone you probably should talk to but aren't quite ready to do so. If this is a Monday, that's always a nice day to start. If it's another day, refer to it as Day One. If you're ready to start today, start as soon as you can. Otherwise start tomorrow. And, hey, this is not a diet, so don't go eating up the whole house today because you're starting up tomorrow. You'll have whatever you want, remember?

Your kitchen is clean. Your journals are ready. Make lists of what you need to get done today. Whether your day begins at home or you're heading to the office, compartmentalize tasks and activities. Write down the names of people you need to call. Make sure your house is clean when you leave it. Straighten out your desk when you first sit down in the morning and when you leave at the end of the day.

Your journal needs to be neat as well. Head the first page of your notebook with the day and date and list the times as you record your information. As you go through your days, this is a good time to begin tracking small events. Tracing responses to people around you and keying in on the parts of your day when you seem to focus more on food. Hungry? Eat. Something else? Separate it out and figure out what you're feeling by simply asking yourself some questions.

What am I feeling? How do I feel about that remark? How do I feel about that plan? What do I want to say to that person? Maybe I should write it down and see if it helps to voice it. Who will I be meeting today and how do I feel around them? Well, I guess you're ready. Kitchen is clean, life is organized (whatever!), notebooks are ready to go. Let's go get some groceries!

Almost Chapter 24

Remember when I told you I didn't name the chapters because I knew you'd run to the food ones? Well, here is *our* moment of truth. You and I are standing in front of the next two chapters and they are all about food. Chapter 24 is a trip to the grocery store. Chapter 25 is all about restaurants. Both chapters are necessary. But is it necessary to read them right now? Or could you come back to them later?

The decision is yours to make. This is the same decision you will need to make anytime you're offered food, or find yourself thinking about food. Just because food is there doesn't mean you have to eat it. Just because there's food in the book doesn't mean you have to read it. You need to start making choices by evaluating your moods, and not just the moods of others.

Personally, I'm not in the mood for food right now. I would much rather be with you! It's food vs. me! Which one of us will you pick? I'll tell you what. I will wait by the entrance to chapter 26. If food talk isn't what you need right now, skip the next two chapters and come back to them later. If food information is what you're hungry for now, read on and find me when you're done. But, hey. Don't get all caught up in the food 'cause I *hate* waiting! I'm gonna start walking . . . you coming?

Chapter 24

I used to wish I could live with someone who was thin, just to keep an eye on her. I wanted to know exactly what she ate, how much, what time, and how often. Because of that, I want to show you what I eat. You may say, "Hey, honey, if you think I want to watch your stupid ass push a cart down aisle five, think again." Or you might want to tag along.

I'll introduce you to some foods you may not have tried and some snack ideas that I like. Later, we'll set up some guidelines, ways to structure the food choices, and I'll show you some of my own personal rituals that always seem to work.

Since I am not a dietitian I can't help you with what your calorie intake should be. It would serve you well to call your doctor and find out. Or pick up a Weight Watchers plan. That's a reputable system that uses points for making your own choices. Remember, though, you're not dieting. You're learning how to eat meals and make your own food decisions. You're learning to eat to your moods as well as to your appetite, which will vary throughout the day.

So here's our shopping list: healthy meal foods, healthy desserts, and healthy snacks, in addition to some unhealthy treats. If we deprive ourselves of junk food, we will cheat on it anyway. Junk food is legal, as long as it is structured. Remember, I do like eating healthfully, but there's always room for Hostess and Doritos. Okay, let's start in the produce section.

Produce. Fruit is full of sugar, and not as full of vitamins as you think. But it's a great snack between meals. I'll often eat an apple before a meal, just to take the edge off my hunger. I've become quite an expert on apples; picking them, preparing them, and finding different ways to enjoy them as a snack. An apple is not a meal.

Granny Smith apples are great cut up, sprinkled with cinnamon and some squirts of light maple syrup. Microwave them until they are soft and warm and have them as a snack. I sometimes put a little milk on top, too. It's really satisfying, warm, sweet, and good. If you like oatmeal, sprinkle it with cinnamon, and add the light syrup and a Granny Smith apple cut up. Microwave or stove-cook it; again, a really great afternoon snack or breakfast.

Cut up your apples, put them in a paper towel, and take them in the car if you're on your way out and feeling a little bit hungry. I'll often do that on the way to lunch or dinner so that I am not famished when I arrive. You do not want to approach a meal starving. Ever.

Cantaloupe is a good one; I eat lots of that when it's in season. For now, stay away from pineapple, watermelon, and honeydew. If you love it, eat it, but watch the quantities. They're pretty steep in calories. This is not a diet! This is information.

We need carrots, celery, and lettuce. Also, cucumbers, tomatoes, pea pods (if you like them in salad), sprouts, and broccoli (try it steamed with a squeeze of fresh lemon and Parmesan cheese sprinkled on top). We need to have as many fresh vegetables as possible. If you don't like them, try whatever you can. Not for diet; for health. You can be thin without vegetables. I want you to be healthy, too.

In the fall, you'll see lots of squashes, which are sweet, filling, and delicious. They are a nice alternative to potatoes and starches but not that low in calories, so be careful of your portions. They're so healthy, and they smell good when they're baking. Eat a quarter of a large squash or a half of a smaller one. Prepare it by slicing it in half, emptying out the seeds, and facing it flesh side down on a baking sheet. Cook at 400 degrees for about an hour or until it's soft. If you need to, add some light syrup or a little brown sugar, but try eating it plain. They are sweet all by themselves. Sometimes I'll have squash for lunch, and sometimes with protein for dinner.

Meat, Poultry, and Fish. Okay, you got through produce. Let's move on to meats. I like the turkey from the deli sliced thick. You can put it in your salad. You can make a sandwich if you like. Try the low-salt, low-fat kind. It really tastes good. If you feel comfortable eating bologna, buy it. I suggest the lower-fat ones, or the turkey bologna. I don't think you'll notice the difference. If you love red meat, buy some. You'll have it for dinner sometimes. Pork chops are lower in fat.

I have a great way for you to make turkey. Buy a breast or a fresh whole one, if you prefer. Place it in a baking pan or tin. Pour apple juice or orange juice on top, and add cut-up onions and carrots and sliced apples with the skin. There is no specific quantity or measurement; it's not like you can mess this one up. If you like, add prunes or any other dried fruit to the bottom of the pan. If you have any around, spoon some frozen orange or apple juice concentrate on top of the turkey before you put it in the oven. Bake it uncovered at 350 degrees until it's done, basting along the way. If you have time, bake at a lower temperature for longer. The juices will turn brown and get much sweeter that way. Begin baking uncovered, and if it starts to get too brown, cover it loosely with foil.

Or put the turkey in a foil pan and cook it on the grill. Put foil on top to cover loosely after it begins to turn brown. The flame should be medium to medium-high. It usually cooks faster here than in the oven, so check it after an hour, basting as you go. The fruit juices will caramelize and the onions will get really sweet. Slice it cold for sandwiches or salads or eat it hot for dinner. My kids love it. That's the way my grandpa cooked turkey and chicken when I was growing up. You can also cook this on the stovetop, in a heavy skillet under low heat. This time, cover it while it cooks. And don't ask me how long to cook it. Just test it until the juices run clear. The longer and slower it cooks the better.

You could also top chicken and turkey on the grill with K.C. Masterpiece marinades. There are many other brands; find the ones that you like. There's a teriyaki flavor and a barbecue flavor, too. The lemon herb is particularly good on the grill. Sometimes I'll mix barbecue sauces with orange marmalade, or some other low-sugar preserves. It sweetens them and gives them a really great flavor without adding more fat. This is not low in sugar, so your "low-carb" diets will not approve. But who says we have to tell them?

Fish is wonderful if you like it. My favorite is grilled or broiled salmon with K.C. Masterpiece or Bull's-Eye barbecue sauce on it. The sauce makes it kind of tangy and sweet and gets caramelized when you cook it. To cook it on the grill, wrap it tightly in foil with lots of sauce spread on top. To test it, open the foil (be careful of the steam) after about ten minutes. If you like it more well done, wait until it's not pink inside. The salmon is also good on top of a salad, cold, the next day.

For company, I buy the large salmon fillets at Costco or Sam's Club and lay them on a sheet of regular aluminum foil with another sheet on top. Then I fold and pinch up the edges all around. They will steam and get bubbly and poached in the foil. These take longer to cook, so check after fifteen minutes. They're so good, they're really inexpensive to serve, and people go nuts over them. You can cook any fish that way. Whitefish is also great steamed in foil on the grill, with fresh lemon and paprika.

Carbohydrates. Yeah, you can eat breads in my house. All these diets tell you to do away with carbs; I believe that should be your decision. If you like carbs and feel deprived without them, here is what you should know. Depriving yourself of them may lead you to overeat them in some of your weaker moments. If you allow yourself to eat them in reasonable amounts, you may find you need them less. I eat them every day and I have 17 percent body fat. That's way low. I try not to make them the larger part of my meal. I balance them with other things, and protein fills me more. If you like them and you feel fine when you eat them, throw them in the cart.

Check at the store for a brand of bread called Natural Ovens, from Manitowoc, Wisconsin. They make a dinner roll that's seventy calories and great to keep in the freezer. I'll have two of them for a snack. There's a low-fat spread that is yogurt-based called Brummel & Brown. I buy it plain but it comes flavored with apple-cinnamon or strawberry if you like. Do your own research with butters and spreads and find the one you like best. I use about a tablespoon or less, just enough for taste. The rolls are good warmed up in the microwave. If you like them sweet, sprinkle them with cinnamon and a little sugar on top of the spread before you heat them. I use sugar and don't overdue artificial sweeteners. I worry about the chemicals. I figure I use enough of them in my hair! They also have a wheat bread that's about sixty or seventy calories a slice. It's great toasted and saves you some calories on a sandwich. Healthy Choice also has decent bread. Any bread you like is fine; don't worry about what kind. The calories per slice don't matter.

On a normal basis, you wouldn't want to have more than four or five servings of bread a day at the most, and you can get along on less. First of all, it has little to no nutritional value. It packs on calories and actually fills you up less than protein ounce for ounce. I try to balance the protein by having it in a sandwich or in a salad. I would recommend that you have at least two or three servings of bread to make sure you're feeding those cravings. Try brown rice, and have you ever tried couscous? It's an interesting and healthy grain that cooks in just five minutes. Sauté onions, mushrooms, and spinach in cooking spray and add to any grain dish.

I have personally given up cereals and it's not because I don't like them. I do. As much as I've gotten to a place where I can eat all kinds of food and keep control over my quantity, cereal is one I still have trouble with and I'll tell you why. A single serving of cereal doesn't satisfy me and having more puts more calories into my breakfast than I want. I'm happier with steamed milk, which fills me, or a waffle that satisfies me. And there's not another time of day that I crave a bowl of cereal. A whole bagel is more than I eat for breakfast, but I would have it for lunch or a three P.M. snack. It's not that I won't eat the calories of that food; I just eat lighter for breakfast since I enjoy a fairly large lunch every day.

You may enjoy a larger breakfast and a somewhat smaller lunch. It's all personal taste and hunger timing. If you like cereal and can get satisfied on a serving, buy it. Get what you like. Frosted Cheerios are not higher in calories than healthier grain cereals. They're also not that healthy. But you get to have things that aren't healthy. Watch out for granola and check the labels. You'll find them ranging from 110 to more than 200 calories per serving. You make the choice. If you love it, it satisfies you, and it's worth the calories to you, then you'll make it up by using a lower-calorie something else in another meal.

In terms of your meals, your hunger, your structure, and your calorie choices, you'll be assessing the hungrier parts of your day. You will decide which meals are bigger by your hunger. There's an old rule: Eat breakfast like a king, lunch like a queen, and dinner like a pauper. I eat breakfast like a queen, lunch like a king (as well as his court), and dinner like a pauper. If you want to eat dinner like a king, then eat dinner like a king. But again, if the reason you eat so much at dinner is because you don't eat all day, you're setting yourself up to overeat. You must eat meals to balance your intake and even out your hunger.

Frozen Foods. I have some favorites here. There's a brand of Belgian waffles by Belgian Chef. They are ninety calories a waffle and are great as a warm, satisfying snack in the late afternoon, or, of course, for breakfast. Top it with light syrup. If one is enough, eat one. If you want to have two, eat two.

For frozen patties, all vegetarian but you can't believe how good, try some or all of these. Boca burgers are meatless burgers made from soy. They also make bratwursts and sloppy joes and they're all terrific. The American classic ("flame grilled") burger has cheese in it and is a little less dry than the original. There are garlic ones, but don't come anywhere near me if you choose those. I can't stand garlic breath! Morningstar Farms makes a pizza burger that I highly recommend. Both of these brands make chicken patties that are also very good. They're all pretty low in fat and very reasonable in calories. They even make corn dogs and chicken nuggets, and my kids like those a lot.

For lunch, I'll have these patties plain or in a sandwich. I use ketchup, barbecue sauce, or mustard. Fill it up with lettuce, tomato, onion; the works if you like. If you want it to seem more like a real fat burger, put two of them together and top it with some low-fat cheese. You'll be adding 150 extra calories to a sandwich that stands somewhere around 300 calories, depending on what you put on it. Doubling the burger and adding cheese puts you at 450. That's not a problem. My lunches are never less than 400 calories, although I try to stay close to that number.

I used to eat vegetables, salads, and fruits for lunch, but I never got satisfied. I prefer to eat something substantial like a sandwich for lunch and eat vegetables with protein for dinner. I eat fruits as snacks in between. If dinner is your hungriest time, you may end up reversing what I do. Make sure, again, that you are not holding back all day in order to allow yourself a large dinner. Don't wait to eat large. The waiting will make you eat more.

I have met many people who say they are not hungry during the day but eat like crazy at night. I tend to think that's because they have trained themselves not to eat all day, and have set a pattern to eat heavily at night. I find that never feels good. A good, healthy, solid lunch feels great. Lots of water all day. And a light dinner feels awesome. When you go to bed you'll feel healthy.

Dairy. I don't go too heavy on dairy because there are some studies that link it to cancer. This is not a recommendation for or against it because I drink vanilla soy milk, and if you have breast cancer that's supposed to be a no-no. I don't know what's right. I do know that in some tribes and in countries where people don't eat dairy there is a lower incidence of cancer. You do your own research, though. I'm no authority; I simply make my own choices as you will.

If you are a dairy person, try a flavored or vanilla yogurt and add some pieces of cut-up apple, banana, raisins, and a few nuts of your choice. It's great around the late afternoon to hold you until your dinner.

You may as well drink skim milk if you're a milk drinker. Like I said, I drink soy milk instead. Why? The FDA says soy is good for your heart. There have been studies that indicate that soy prevents certain cancers. But, then again, new studies have said that soy may not be worth all the hype. It feels healthy, though. And because it's vanilla and sweet, I find it richer and better-tasting than milk. So I have to take this opportunity to ask you to try something. It happens to be one of my bigger, fancier secrets and has saved me a lot of calories while filling me up. Remember flexibility? Keep an open mind here before you say no.

Everyone loves the lattes and cappuccinos at Starbucks, right? That's a nice way to get your calcium and it fills you up more than a cup of coffee. But I realized that all of that coffee was staining my teeth. I didn't want to drink so much milk, so I asked for one of their soy steamers, which is vanilla-flavored soy milk, steamed and frothy. It has about the same calories as skim milk and the same amount of calcium. But if you prefer to have milk, then have milk. Add their flavorings if you like. They are very filling and satisfying.

If you're running around and find yourself hungry, it holds you over until your next meal.

If you're still with me I have to tell you the next step. I was spending too much money at Starbucks but didn't want to give up the habit. So I bought my own espresso steamer from their store. I tried many brands and found that I liked vanilla Sun Soy and vanilla Silk the best. They are both sweet but I add a sweetener, too. I have it every morning and sometimes later in the day as a snack. Even my daughter likes it and she's human. Scott likes it and he was more skeptical than you.

Cheese. Whether you eat cheese is up to you. If you love it, get it. If you're okay with lower-fat cheeses, get them. Mozzarella, feta, and blue cheese come in skim varieties, and I like them in my salads. High-fat ones are fine, too, but consider buying the cheese shredded. It will flavor things with less cheese per square foot. You'll begin to decide where you want to put your calories and where you want to save them. As you look at foods, and I'm not talking Doritos and doughnuts, I'm talking meals, decide what you love and buy it. Soy cheeses are worth trying, too.

Canned Food. I don't buy it. I am not a cat. But if you like canned foods, then buy them.

Salads and Salad Dressings. They are full of calories, even if you use the low-fat ones. In order to get a lot of flavor, you need to use quite a bit. So here's what I suggest. If you like salad, eat salad. If you eat salad to lose weight, give it up. You're better off eating a sandwich. For a healthy side dish, dip raw vegetables in a bit of dressing.

I ate salads for years and didn't lose weight. They are the dieting myth. Don't eat them to diet. Eat them because they are fresh and filling and complement any meal. Try buying rice vinegar. It's sweet, flavorful, and twenty-five calories a tablespoon. Some rice vinegars have no calories but they won't taste as good. Use a tablespoon or two of your low-fat dressing and add a tablespoon or two of the rice vinegar. It will cut the thickness of the dressing and add a lot of flavor. Try balsamic vinegar, too. It has a strong, rich flavor. Often I combine the two vinegars, add Parmesan cheese, and skip any other dressing.

One day when you're at home, measure one tablespoon of dressing. Typically, two tablespoons equals one serving. You need to see what a small amount that is. If you can get in the habit of using less dressing, you will save a lot of calories. Here are some more ideas to make the salad taste great.

Try adding chopped apples, pears, mangoes, or tangerines; add raisins or dried cranberries; and try sprinkling a few nuts. And maybe some low-fat feta cheese. Canned beets are sweet, too. Fresh basil is sold in the produce section. Cut the leaves and throw them in the salad for a fresh, pungent flavor. The more flavors you add to your salad, the less salad dressing you'll need. Try broccoli slaw. It's shredded like coleslaw, and very crunchy with an interesting texture. Here's a recipe for Chinese cole slaw that you'll love.

You'll need 2 packages of broccoli slaw, 2 packages of chicken ramen soup mix, ½ cup of red wine vinegar, 1 cup of canola oil (that's what the recipe calls for, but I try to use ½ cup of oil), ½ cup of sugar, and 1 small package of slivered almonds. Add 5 chopped green onions if you like (onion breath is a close second to garlic, you know). Mix the slaw with the soup mix, liquids, sugar, and almonds. Break the ramen noodles and add them to the salad with the seasoning packets. Mix it all up. This can sit in the fridge for days and is better when it's made an hour or so in advance. Depending on how much oil you use, this salad can be rather high in calories, so I would eat it as a side dish to something else.

Fats. Fats are an important part of our diet. Without them we can't get satisfied. Without them we won't stay healthy. I eat fats, but I don't eat only the healthy ones. I eat the unhealthy ones, too. Right or wrong, here's what I do and you'll do what works for you.

I enjoy eating healthy foods. They probably make up 85 percent of what I consume overall. If I have too much junk food, I crave days of only vegetables and fruits. In order to maintain the 85 percent healthy part of my eating, the other 15 percent of my diet has to be fantastic. In terms of calories or fat content, I won't waste that 15 percent on anything short of something that I love. I am very picky in this area. For example, I love cold butter on bread in a restaurant, but if something is cooked in butter I won't eat it. I hate olive oil, too. I don't like slippery food. I will always cook fish and omelets dry or in cooking spray. When I am in a restaurant, I order things dry as well. If it comes swimming in oil, I will send it back. I won't waste my 15 percent. Here's the way I spend it:

I save my calories from slip-and-slide food and put it into treats and desserts. I love cake and cookies, and not the low-fat kinds either. Ice cream is not my favorite; it borders on slippery. I like texture and density in my confections. Just hand me some frozen pound cake and there's my fat for the day.

Every day I have fat in a treat. Sometimes it is a healthy treat, like a peanut butter and jelly sandwich, something I never used to allow myself. Or I will add nuts and raisins to a salad or yogurt. Sometimes I will eat real mayonnaise instead of eating a sandwich with mustard, which has no fat. But I ain't wasting it on olive oil just because it's the "healthy fat"! *But,* if you love olive oil and cake does nothing for you, slip slide away!

On the days my fats are more on the healthy side but still substantial in calories, like a great sandwich, I will still crave something "dessert." I will pop a couple of Junior Mints, or a Halloween-size candy bar. Many days it's a Hostess Ho Ho. Let me tell you something about Ho Hos. They are junky, no doubt. They are also packaged individually and just enough to satisfy me without overwhelming calories. Try keeping them cold in the fridge. Ho Ho Ho!

Crunchy Stuff. Well, I recommend air-popped popcorn, or microwave light popcorn. I am a huge fan of flavored rice cakes, especially the white cheddar ones. They are very salty, so when I crave salt, they always do the trick. I keep them around for snacks, and if I'm in trouble I figure they do a lot less damage than chips.

For the days I do want chips, I keep those lunch-bag sizes around. One bag of nacho cheese Doritos has less than 150 calories. I don't ever eat out of a large bag where I lose track of the quantity. Pretzels are low in fat and crunchy, but for some reason they don't do it for me. I stay away from nuts as a snack because they are so high in calories, but use them as a condiment in salads, in yogurt, or on top of frozen yogurt. They are a healthy form of protein and fat if used in small servings.

If crunch is what you want, you can try eating vegetables. Snap peas, celery, and red and yellow peppers are nice alone or dipped. There are low-fat dips and dressings, but go light on the amounts. Jicama, if you're not familiar with it, is a Mexican vegetable that looks like a mutant potato. You'll find it at most grocery stores. Just peel it and slice it into sticks or wedges. It is sweet, crunchy, and very good to munch on. By the way, when I make a salad, all of these crunchy vegetables go in it.

Desserts. When shopping for your desserts, get what you feel safe having around and protect yourself in the event of a binge. You don't want huge bags of cookies around if you can't feel safe. Low-fat puddings are good, prepackaged and portioned.

There are a couple of new brands of round ice cream sandwiches that are fabulous, such as the "Skinny Cow," made by Silhouette. They are about 120 calories each. Healthy Choice makes low-fat ice cream that's good; 120 calories per half-cup. Edy's Grand makes a chocolate ice cream for 150 calories and that's good, too. You'll also find fruit-juice bars, sorbets, and fudge bars, all low in calories and fats. If they satisfy you, that's great. To me, they taste like diet food.

Make your decisions from cravings and safety combined. If you don't think you can control yourself around certain foods, stay with the ones that feel safe for now. One day, when you're in the same place I am today, you will feel safe with them all.

Cookies are a good dessert. The problem is that for now it may not be wise for you to have them around. Eating a couple of cookies is something you'll do in graduate school, not where you are today. I learned something interesting about cookies. If you are in a good place, you can have one or a couple and stop there. If you're in a marginal or bad place, stopping means you reached into the box and felt your fingers hit bottom. Always a bad place, that bottom of the box.

I used to buy SnackWell's cookies because they were very low in fat and they tasted pretty good. But psychologically, because I considered them "diet cookies," I would tend to overeat them. If you feel safer with them, then buy them. But let me tell you where I am today with my cookies.

What I have found is that if I have big cookies around, and I mean those large one-hundred- to two-hundred-calorie cookies, I will eat one but usually not two. If the cookies are small, I tend to keep eating them. I have even started, every once and a while, going to 7-Eleven to buy these large frosted cookies with Spider-Man or smiley faces on them. I will eat the whole thing, which has to be at least three hundred calories and maybe quite a bit more.

What's interesting is that for those three hundred calories I get a very full, satisfying dose of cookie, which has a beginning and an end. It's not out of control, and when it's done it's done. I let myself say yes to a big cookie and finish it instead of saying no to a bunch of smaller or low-fat cookies that I need to finish or overeat. I'm guessing I've saved myself hundreds of potential calories, time and time again. And it's a fantasy come true to eat a big, fat cookie just because I want to.

A great snack and dessert combination are protein bars. I have tried many of them, but Zone Perfect bars are my favorite. They taste like a grown-up Rice Krispies treat. There is a large selection of flavors, but I am partial to the chocolate–peanut butter and the fudge grahams. Here's the trick. Take a bite and gulp down lots of water. After every bite I take, I drink from my water bottle. It is not only very filling, but it gets my water in. Drinking lots of water is key to keeping your weight down and keeping your body healthy. If I am on the run and know I won't have time to eat, I keep Zone Perfect bars in the car or in my purse. They take the edge off a meal that's late. If I don't have time for a meal, and there's no fruit around to eat with it, I will eat two. One bar is not enough for a meal.

Viactiv is a calcium chew. It comes in several different flavors: chocolate, caramel, mocha, and fruit. Each has twenty calories and five hundred milligrams of calcium. I eat three a day. They satisfy my sweet tooth a lot of the time. I keep some in my purse and pop one after a meal if I'm out. They put a finish on it for me. After I have one, I often brush my teeth. Not only do they stick to my teeth, but it sends the signal to me that I'm done. Because of the calcium, two or more at once gives me a stomachache. Eat them one at a time, at different times of the day.

If you are a candy lover, try keeping Halloween-size candy bars in your freezer; they make a great small dessert and last longer when they are frozen. If you don't feel safe, put a few in the freezer for practice and give the rest of the bag to someone else or throw it out. The two bucks wasted is wasted in the garbage with a lot less damage than the waste when it goes into your mouth. Never second-guess throwing out unsafe food or food you don't want to finish.

As you walk down the aisles of the supermarket, look for foods that seem healthy and interesting; not over-the-top, boring diet foods and not over-the-top junk either. If you look at a food and begin to feel you could not stop eating it, don't buy it. For right now you're playing it safe. But make the foods ones you'll enjoy.

Now that we've organized your kitchen and stocked it full of safe food, what happens when someone utters the words "Let's go out for dinner"?

Chapter 25

There's a fear we all have of restaurants because we know we'll overeat. There are too many temptations, like bread baskets and sweet butter, rich-tasting entrées, and fabulous desserts. The portions, if large, are hard not to finish and the whole experience is rough. We always gain weight from eating out. In addition, we've been told what to order if we want to keep our weight low: fish dry, salad bare, everything on the side, skip dessert, and don't touch anything good. WRONG!

Certainly, ordering healthy food that is reasonably low in fat is a great way to go. But if you order food you don't like or that leaves you feeling deprived, you are in danger of overeating or bingeing. Fattening food does not make you fat. Stuffing yourself full of diet food can. I know I am repeating myself, but I cannot say it enough. I lost weight when I decided to eat. The more choices I allowed myself, the less quantity I needed.

As I mentioned before, I have learned to enjoy the taste of foods that are prepared without butter and oil. It was not hard for me to give that up because I chose to put the calories elsewhere. In every meal I have, though, I need to choose something that I truly want. There are ways I compromise. Can I have every item on the menu? Well, kind of.

For all of the years I went to restaurants and didn't get what I wanted, I am making up for that today. This may sound eccentric to you, but to me it's just enjoying my freedom. Often, I will order several things so I can have tastes of them all. If we're out for breakfast and I want an omelet but I feel like pancakes, too, I order them both. Or I will ask Scott to split two or three things with me and we decide what sounds good to us both. I know what you're thinking. How do you not overeat? You may overeat at the beginning because you'll be so excited that you're allowing yourself what you want. But once you get over the novelty of this exciting new privilege, you'll just eat a part of each and leave the rest behind. If you want to be protective, ask for to-go containers as soon as they bring the food. The moment you know you have had enough, put the rest away. You can have it later when you are hungry.

If you are not ready for that yet, let's deal with feeding cravings in a healthy, satisfying manner. Let's use the 85 percent rule. Let the bigger portion of what you order be healthy. Let the smaller part, the 15 percent, feel like a treat. Using my example above, you could order an egg-white omelet with veggies cooked dry. You could skip the hash browns and ask for sliced tomatoes. Since eggs usually come with toast, you could ask for a side of pancakes instead, and maybe eat half of them. That meal is 85 percent healthy with a treat served on the side. If toast is more what you crave, eat one piece instead of two. Half of a bagel with marmalade is another treat you could have. If you want cheese in your omelet, that adds fat and calories and it also fills you up. You may not want anything else.

At lunch you could order a salad with veggies and chicken. The 85 percent healthy rule leaves you room for a roll or two with butter. If it's a sandwich you've ordered, perhaps it's a higher-calorie sandwich that includes bread, protein, and fat. The 85 percent and the 15 percent are both inside the meal. End the meal with a small piece of candy or have a calcium chew.

Let's say you are in the mood for a rather large and rich dessert and you long for more than 15 percent. Your best bet is to satisfy some of your hunger on something healthy. You will make the controlled decision to eat lightly at your meal in order to save up for dessert. Eating that light meal will not feel like deprivation, it will feel like a smart compromise. You don't want a sliver. You're in the mood for a hunk. Let me tell you what I do.

I am a lover of chocolate cake. I like the kind that is really high, really dense, and needs to be served with a butcher knife to cut it. There is one restaurant in particular that has this type of cake. When we go there I order a salad with plain balsamic vinegar and Parmesan cheese. I eat one of the rolls and wait to enjoy my dessert. But I used to do the same thing you do. You know what you do. When cakes or pies are offered, even at someone's home, you take a pathetic sliver.

How many skinny slivers of cake with your stupid skinny knife does it take to equal my hunk of wonder with my ax? I'll bet you *anything,* your slivers outweigh my hunk any day of the weekend. I walk away satisfied; do you? I walk *away;* do you? I made the decision to go light on my meal, and then I felt entitled to have it.

Make smart choices. There will be days you don't feel like that piece of cake. Not because you can't, but because there are other things you're more in the mood for. Maybe you could easily give up dessert but would love some mashed potatoes, or a pasta dish you adore. Maybe you feel like a nice, juicy steak. So when the bread basket comes you will compromise since you know those potatoes are coming. And to balance the food healthfully, you'll start off with a fresh, light salad. Still afraid to order food that sounds so good? Don't forget the math we did with overeating. You are dividing it in half. Half goes to enjoying food and the other half goes to weight loss.

Your body and brain will crave a balance if you allow it. If you have one rich meal, it doesn't mean you won't stop. But if you never allow it and you don't satisfy your cravings with the *actual* food you crave, you won't be able to stop. If you've had the attitude that going to restaurants makes you gain weight, let it go. You can eat out as often as you like.

Let me tell you about my dog. Snickers is a friendly, very large golden retriever puppy. He's almost two years old. He used to be so excited to be around us that he wouldn't give us any space and he was irritating the crap out of us. We began to put him behind dog gates so we could watch TV without his slobber all over our laps. The more we put him away, the more out of control he got when we allowed him back in the room. Snickers wanted us. Snickers was deprived of us. Snickers was bingeing on us and he couldn't stop because he knew he would later be rationed.

Snickers created his own problem. I mean, he's a dog and I can't blame him, but we can all learn from his actions. He simply wanted to be with us and that was something he should have had. But he overdid it and then couldn't have it at all. Being told he couldn't have it made him lose control. Losing control made him lose the privilege of having the very thing he wanted.

We finally got smart. We never put him away anymore. We just let him be around us and now that dog is calm. His out-of-control need for us is gone. He sits on the floor quietly beside us and we can't believe he's the same dog. Still slobbers, though.

Being told you can't have something makes you need it more. Being told you *can* have it makes you need it less and allows you to be calm within that need. I want you to remember Snickers every time you go to a restaurant. Don't look at the menu to decide what you should have. Look and decide what you want. If you are allowed to have exactly what you want, your need for it will grow smaller.

Let's look at casual dining. Fast foods are what we consider unthinkable for weight loss or maintenance. Not true at all. On days you find yourself in that setting, there are reasonable choices that you can make. Every time I used to go to a fast-food place and didn't order food because I thought I would never lose weight if I did, I ended up either picking or overeating when I got home. Stop picking at your kid's fries and crusts and start ordering food for yourself!

Fast-food chains. You can have it. McDonald's, Burger King, and Wendy's have salads with grilled chicken. Go easy on the dressing. Order a grilled chicken sandwich without the mayo and put barbecue sauce on it instead. Wendy's has baked potatoes, and they're good with broccoli and squeezed lemon. Ask them to hold the butter since they can scoop it on pretty heavy. Have butter if you like, but try it without as well.

Pizza. Did you ever try ordering pizza without cheese? It's actually very good. Order it with extra sauce, lots of veggies, and thin crust if you've had some bread that day, thick crust if you haven't. If you order it with the cheese, it's also fine; take half the cheese off. You don't need so much. No, you don't!

Chinese food. I won't tell you to avoid foods except for this one unless you love it. It swims in oil, floats in sodium, and portioning here is vague. If you are going to eat it, then have it in small amounts. And never weigh yourself the next day; you'll hold enough water to fill a pool. You can request that it be cooked without oil, but even their broths are so full of salt. I stay away from it completely, but if you want it, eat it. Ask the waiter for lighter options on the menu in terms of fat and salt.

Breakfast places. Egg-white omelets. All of my friends and family have seen the light of my whites. There is not one of my friends I haven't turned on to these golden nuggets of weight management. They are fluffy. They are filling. They are so low in calories and they are delicious. Order them cooked in Pam or dry, with broccoli, spinach, tomatoes, and onions; mushrooms are good on them, too. Skip the hash browns and order fruit or tomato slices instead. Eat half a bagel or a piece of toast. It's a winning lunch or dinner.

Now that I'm not afraid of it, I order my omelet with cheese. If I do that I skip the bread. Most places that specialize in breakfasts have fluffy omelets. If you try a place and they don't, try another. If you ever come to Chicago, you must go to Mitchell's on Clybourn and ask for the owner. His name is Taki and over the years we have become family. I once went into the kitchen to kiss the man who makes these enormous fluffy creations. He was a great big black man with a smile that lit the ovens. When he tried to pass one off on me that was not quite the size I expected, I sent it back and told him never to make me a "white-boy omelet" again. After that he started sending me two. If you don't live here in Chicago, I'd make plans to visit soon.

It still amazes me that all of the years I went to restaurants and ordered vegetable plates or salads without dressing, I never lost weight. Now I see that because I wasn't looking forward to what I had ordered, I filled up on bread and dessert. Or I would eat all day in anticipation of ordering food that was boring. I graduated to ordering boring fish as an entrée; at least it was a meal. I'd finish the fish, still eat the bread, and indulge in too much dessert.

Today, I order whatever it is I want. I've watched everyone's mouths fall open when I ordered a New York strip. "Nancy's eating meat!" I now look forward to it and save myself. Not by starving myself, I know better than to do that, but by eating a little bit lighter. This is weight management.

I'll often have an apple sometime before leaving for the restaurant, or I'll have a Zone Perfect bar with lots of water late in the afternoon. I don't want to arrive there starving. I will always have some of the bread because it tastes good, not because I have ordered nothing else that does. Smaller amounts satisfy me, words I never believed I would say.

I'm not going to tell you that I frivolously order whatever rich, buttery, cream-laden entrée I want. I don't and they don't really appeal to me. I could have a taste of someone else's, and that would be enough. You know why? I never feel well after I eat them. I don't like the feeling of leaving a meal full and sick to my stomach.

Here are some other restaurant tips. If you have a salad as an entrée or as a side, ask for plain balsamic vinegar and Parmesan cheese on the side. Remember that the vinegar has a full and strong taste, so don't go too heavy to start. If you use their regular dressing, dip your empty fork into the dressing, and then scoop up some salad. You'll use very little dressing this way. If you love the rich dressing and love it poured on the salad, then have it. But go lighter somewhere else. Remember, this is all about making your own food and calorie choices. Whatever feels right to you is right for you.

The bread: Eat it. Put some butter on it if you like. Maybe for lunch that day you'll have a salad with chicken and turkey instead of a sandwich because you know you'll have bread when you're out that night. Or maybe you'll have a sandwich and skip the bread at the restaurant. You'll play around with the combinations that work best for you.

The entrée should absolutely be whatever you're in the mood to have. If you order fettuccine Alfredo, start out with a salad. I believe you'll eat less overall simply because you ordered what you wanted. But I understand your fear. Because it tastes so good, you're afraid you'll never stop and that will make you gain weight.

How could anyone have a small portion of something that tastes so good? Simple. They just stop when they are no longer hungry. What a concept, huh?

As the half-eaten plate of food sits in front of you, cue into your physical self. At that moment you have eaten something great and you feel satisfied but not full. You feel like you could certainly eat more and you're beginning to feel nervous about not being able to stop. The mere fact that you're thinking about it tells you that you are moving away from hunger and entering the place of "enough."

Take another bite. Are you feeding hunger or does it just taste good? You need to make a choice. Either the food is just too good to pass up and it's worth it to you to feel uncomfortable in exchange for the enjoyment of eating, *or* you make another decision. You would rather not overeat and you'd like to leave the meal feeling comfortable.

No one is telling you to stop. If you want more you will have more. But begin to recall the feeling of leaving a meal feeling full, uncomfortable, and kind of slow-moving. Then imagine walking away from the table with a belt that doesn't need to be loosened, and a mood that has no regret. There's a pride in walking away from food that you really didn't need to eat.

Put your hand on your stomach. It is not distended beyond what it was when you sat down. Sit up straight. Feel your healthy posture not having to shift around with that discomfort from being full. And finally, give yourself a mental pat on the back. You made a strong decision not to make yourself feel uncomfortable.

If you make the decision to eat it, then do that and enjoy the food. Today is a day you chose to eat more than you needed. Examine it. Was there something else going on? Use the tools we've discussed with SAFE, Separate Always Food and Emotion. It's possible that there was nothing emotional going on and this is a day you ate more than usual. You can have days like that and still eat less overall during the week. That means weight loss even when there are days you eat more.

Sounds so easy, right? We both know it sounds impossible. It's hard, all right, but it's very possible. Here are some hints to help it happen. Ask the waiter to clear your plate and decide on that doggie bag. If you can carry a small travel toothbrush, disappear to the bathroom and brush your teeth. You can also pop a mint or a piece of gum into your mouth. You could order a cup of coffee or tea, another end-of-a-meal habit. I carry those chocolate calcium chews with me. Having something sweet, for me, puts an end to my meal.

Imagine coming back home after a meal like that. Not that full but totally satisfied. Imagine not needing anything more to eat. Want to know my favorite Dionne Warwick song that describes what you'll do in the kitchen? "Walk On By."

Chapter 26

Hi, honey! I'm not even going to ask you. You know I'm dying to know if you stopped at those chapters or if you came right here. But remember, I just won't judge you. Good friends never do that. Oh, I can't stand it. Was I your first choice or was food your first choice? Okay, fine, whatever. But listen to what happened to me.

We were spending the summer in our house in the country. My older son's best friends came to spend a few days with us. Between my three children, their friends, and the neighborhood kids, it was not unusual for there to be ten kids there, and sometimes quite a few more. I love when my house is full.

On Saturday, Scott and I took some of the kids for a very long bike ride and we stopped at a place for lunch. I thought about you and my history when I sat down at this restaurant. I used to go there and not eat their food since I thought it was too fattening. I would have had to eat at home before we went, or later after we returned. Sometimes I would order one of their bad salads and pick off everyone's plates.

On this day, however, I looked over the menu with a sort of joy in realizing how far I'd come. I looked to see what I was in the mood for, reflecting on all of the restaurant tips I've discussed with you. I ordered a grilled chicken sandwich with barbecue sauce. I wouldn't have done that in the past because it would have sounded too fattening. I always wanted a sandwich but knew it would be gone in two bites. Salads looked bigger on the plate and took longer to eat. What I knew that day was that a nice big sandwich was what I craved.

I was very hungry. I had run that morning and followed it with the bike ride. It was hot outside. I was totally looking forward to the big fat chicken sandwich that was being cooked at that very moment.

There were some men walking into the restaurant on a scavenger hunt, looking for waitresses with clues, and I was busy telling the kids what they were doing. I told them about the scavenger hunt I had made for the town's "Adult Night" a few summers earlier. One of the clues sent the groups to a skanky motel where they had to get the key to room number 8. They were instructed to knock on the door for their clue. I had planted a guy there, watching TV in bed, and told him to answer the door as though he were staying there. We were engrossed in our fun conversation until finally our food came. Here I was doing everything right.

I opened the sandwich, which came with chips (I said no to the fries when asked), ready to put the tomato on. I took a look at the chicken that was to be my well-deserved lunch and wondered what ant it would fill, 'cause it sure as hell wouldn't fill me. I ate that pathetic excuse for a sandwich and was left with one single need. More. I ate the chips, ate my kids' fries, and then ate their friends' fries, too. Finally I was full, but I was also quite disgusted. I will tell you that I didn't sweat it, though. I figured I'd eat light at dinner.

We ended up at the beach for a couple of hours, then headed back home. Everyone was hot and tired. I commented to Scott what a great day it had been, but now I was ready to relax. As we approached the house we saw our friends and their kids standing on our porch. What lucky timing, we all chanted; they had just come by for a swim.

I was not unhappy they were there, but I would have loved just a bit of downtime. I wasn't in the mood to entertain. Everyone was hanging out by the pool, and as I passed through the kitchen, there they were. Homemade cookies that Scott had brought home from a friend who knows he loves them. Cookies that I had turned down the night before. But that was then, this was now; this was another day. I offered them to our guests, as any good hostess would, and then devoured the rest myself.

Okay, I thought, so maybe that wasn't the light dinner I had imagined as a follow-up to the chips and fries. But you know me, I would never skip a meal due to poor eating before, so I decided, "Hey, why wait?" I opened up last night's turkey, and had a couple of chocolate-covered grahams. I quickly snarfed it down while I watched everyone through the kitchen window. I went to brush my teeth, and joined the group outside. I could tell you this is where it ended, now that I am valedictorian of the University of Binge-a-Soda. But, then, I would be lying to you.

Several hours later, after I had chosen not to eat the pizza we ordered, which was a very disciplined and right-choice move, after I had said no to the ice cream that everyone else was having, and after I cleaned up the plates and garbage, I decided I really did hate my marriage and found myself some more food. What had happened to trigger that feeling? I'm not sure I could have tracked it, I just know that the feeling was there. But bear with me as I make a connection.

In the Jewish religion, we have a tradition following the death of a family member. It's called sitting shivah. After the funeral service everyone gathers at the home of the bereaved to spend time, offering their love and support. And, of course, to stuff themselves with food. People always bring food to a shivah house. And there's an order to how this is done.

Custom has it that someone other than the closest grieving family member orders deli trays of large quantity while others cook, bake, and bring. The mood is not heavy or depressing at all since the funeral served that purpose. This is a time to laugh, converse, share memories, look at pictures, and remember. With love, humor, and joy. With a bagel, some lox, and some kugel. With some fruit, some coffee, and cake. Or any of the thirty baked goods that have been baked by loving friends.

Someone will send a dinner for that evening, sometimes even set it up and serve it. Then they will clean it up. Everything that is offered to the family is offered in conjunction with food. *Everything!* With the exception of the hugs, words, attentive ears, and presence, the food is the major event. And let me tell you how major.

Shivah traditionally goes on for up to seven days. Each of those days, fresh food is brought in, and the quantity is for much more than the immediate family, since they will typically have friends and extended family joining. Every day, platters, tins, and trays come in. And more and more home-baked desserts. Nothing gets thrown away. Jews don't throw away food. Where I live, they buy extra refrigerators and freezers and keep them in their basements. Why do you think Jews need basements? Actually, they need garages, too, sized for two and a half cars. Have you ever seen half of a car? It's space for two cars and a fridge.

It's a loving, supportive time. It's a time when friends and family provide. It's truly a beautiful custom, and to be on the receiving end of everyone's coming together for you is a heartwarming and fulfilling experience. It does exactly what it sets out to do. It makes you feel that although the pain is horrible, you're not left alone to feel it. You have others to help you through.

The hardest part of the mourning does not take place during shivah. Not during those days of distractions, in a house full of chatter and life. The hardest time is after. When everyone goes back to their homes and the food has all been put away. When everything is quiet, so very quiet, and you sit alone with the loss.

That's the shivah custom and it applies only to the death of a person. The end of someone's life. What about the endings that have nothing to do with death? Those that are inside of life? It does not need to be the death of something huge but one that feels huge at the moment. It could be the death of an idea, the death of a desire, the death of a hope, or the death of an image. Or maybe it's just an ending. And it may not be a bad one; simply one that brings on emotion. The end of your child's first year of school. The end of a job that you're ready and choosing to leave. The end of a party or event you've been planning for months or years. And maybe it needs to be felt. Perhaps it needs to be mourned. Maybe we all need to sit shivah for the smaller moments in life. For the passing of an event. For the passing of an emotion.

When we experience the loss or end of a something, there needs to be a custom to grieve it. Sometimes the food can help by providing an action. Sometimes we need to share it and surround ourselves with others. And as much as we don't want to be left alone with that pain, at some point we need to face it. Without the friends, without the sounds of people, and without the commotion of food. We need to suffer through that pain. It's a natural part of life.

Life has pain. Terrible, gut-wrenching, knifelike, and agonizing. There's simply no way to avoid its existence in who we are as people. We can try to cover it, conceal it, talk ourselves out of it, and find things to take our attention away from it. We can take antidepressants and let that make us feel better. That is fine for many, but there is a downside to that. It may make us believe we can't survive the pain without it. Pain isn't something we want. But if it comes and we turn it around, it may bring something magical.

The days that I learned to face pain, I learned what pain really feels like. It was so awful, I knew why I had avoided it for so long. But something else came with it. The belly-gripping laughs that had been missing in my life, the over-the-top silliness that I used to have as a child. When I opened myself to the pain, I opened myself to life. It was a natural progression, nothing I had to force. It brought me some things that I really don't like. But it brought my strength to the top.

My barricades had been food. It was all that I could see. When I stopped treating pain like something I wasn't supposed to have, I learned I could handle it. I learned that as bad as any moment can get, that moment will always pass.

At every shivah house is a bowl of hard-boiled eggs. Eggs represent life and birth. To me, they represent something more. Separating the yolk from the white is what gives me my egg-white omelets. And it gives me an analogy for you. Separate food and emotion. Separate feelings from life. Life can be happy and good while feelings are bad and painful. If you feel sad and pained, it doesn't mean your life is bad. And if you feel happy and joyful, it doesn't mean pain isn't there. It's all there. Encased in the shell of the egg. Encased in the one life you have.

That night I hated my marriage. It doesn't make it all bad. The next night we watched a sunset. That didn't make it all good. But in that moment in my kitchen, whatever I felt, it had really gotten to me. I went and ate Carol's cookies. I should have just gone and cried.

But, then again, there ain't nothing wrong with Carol's cookies. Especially the ones with chips. And shivah food is always good, but only for so long. You want to hear something else, another part of the custom? You're never supposed to take food out of a shivah house. The theory is it could bring bad luck. I'm not sure what kind of bad luck, but I suspect it might be weight gain.

Oh, my, I lost all track of time. I'd love to tell you more. But I think it's time for breakfast.

Chapter 27

I believe breakfast is your most important meal and I don't mean nutritionally. It sets your tone for the entire day. If you start off with a large, high-calorie, unhealthy breakfast, you start off sluggish. If you eat nothing, you set yourself up for a deeper hunger later. You also lose the advantage of the one meal that gets burned off in the natural course of your day, no matter what.

Most people who don't eat breakfast don't want to spend the calories. That's okay. I'm not asking you to eat a lot. Have something if for no other reason than that it sets up a pattern of structure, which is the key to losing weight.

I'll give you a sliding pass here if you want to go on to the next chapter and eat breakfast on the run. If you're not in the mood for food talk, don't let *me* hold you up. Just make sure you eat it, okay? But listen up. Sometimes the reason we overeat is because we let ourselves get too hungry. Often we don't even realize it until we sit down to eat. If you decide to skip the food talk, just remember that point. See ya up ahead.

As I told you before, my breakfast is light because that's when I have my steamed soy milk. I have a little more than a cup, which equals about 140 calories. Because it's hot and frothy, it always fills me up. That's not enough for breakfast by most people's standards, but I eat a lunch that is larger than most people's standards. Remember, this is individual choice and need. You'll play around with amounts that feel right in each of your meals, but don't make the mistake of having nothing.

Midmorning I'll have some fruit. I try to keep to a maximum of three hundred calories before lunch. More than that seems like too much for me. If you want to stay in that calorie range, here are some decent options that I choose from. You should certainly explore others if there's nothing here that you like. For a man, you may need to add to this, or combine some of the selections. You can find out your recommended calorie intake by asking your doctor or nutritionist.

- Waffles (Two brings you to around two hundred calories; adding light syrup and/or Brummel & Brown spread will bring you up to three hundred. Have one if that seems like enough, but there's nothing wrong with two.)
- One cup of steamed soy or milk, or one cup of yogurt with fruit. One cup of blueberries has one hundred calories. Strawberries can be as much as twenty-five calories each if they're large. Fruit has lots of sugar, so don't go crazy with it.
- Two pieces of toast with margarine or butter and some fruit
- A bagel (try having half of one) with cream cheese or margarine, along with some sort of fruit
- Oatmeal with cinnamon, apples, and light syrup
- Egg whites in an omelet or scrambled with low-fat cheese and veggies. Cook them in a cooking spray and don't spray the bajeebers out of it. Those sprays are not calorie-free in excess. Have a piece of toast or fruit. Egg whites have only fifteen calories each; I use six in an omelet.
- Cereal of your choice. Measure out the serving suggested; cereals really add up.
- Breakfast bars or Zone Perfect bars are great when you're in a hurry.
- Try drinking hot water with lemon instead of coffee or juice. I lost you there, didn't I? Really, though, you can never have too much water, and having it hot is rather nice.

If you like to have juice in the morning, there's nothing wrong with that. Just a point of information: Juice has quite a few calories per serving. In most cases you could have two pieces of fruit for the same calories as one glass of juice. Try drinking water instead of juice and eat a piece of fruit. The fruit is more substantial and you get more of the fiber when you eat the whole piece. Fiber is not only good for you, it also fills you up.

If you are a coffee drinker, fine. I have never developed the caffeine habit. If you want to try a day without it, wait a few days, until you've found yourself some structure. I would be curious to see, once you tap into a healthier feeling about your body, if you don't find that energy and awakeness comes from you and not the coffee. However, I have heard that it's best not to quit cold turkey. Perhaps you could mix half decaf and half regular in the beginning to avoid headaches from withdrawal.

The above items are chosen in the name of structure, foods with a beginning and an end. If you want a muffin or strudel, I won't try to stop you, but have an awareness of eating lightly and healthfully. That kind of food may serve better as a dessert or alongside a light lunch. Lots of sugar at breakfast won't feel healthy and sets up a sweet-tooth signal for hours.

I implore you not to miss breakfast. I never, ever skip it. I pay for it if I do and it totally throws off my day. If you are fed regularly, but not overfed, your body will operate efficiently. Psychologically, you've started your day feeding and not depriving. Feeding but not overeating. Making choices with foods that are healthy, satisfying, and not so very heavy. That is a strong way to start your day.

You could read the paper now. We could sit here and just not talk. You could obsess about breakfast and if you've made the right choice for our first day on the Bod Squad. You could write in your journal. Tell me what you're thinking. C'mon, I've told you so much stuff here. I promise I won't tell. Who would I ever tell anyway? I still don't know your name!

Chapter 28

Somewhere between the not-so-distant past and the very recent past, I was in the middle of something that I didn't know how to survive. I'm not being dramatic; I didn't know how to live my life anymore. Everyone in my family was perfectly healthy. Money wasn't a problem and we had more than ever before. What was happening was so terribly painful that every morning I woke up I wondered how I would make it.

The simple motion of swinging my legs from under the covers of my bed was the hardest part of the day. Putting my feet on the floor meant the acceptance of another day in a life I no longer wanted to live.

I have certain spots in my emotional makeup, certain weaknesses that when triggered are extremely painful. Just as our bodies are more tender in some spots than others; a kick in one place can hurt, a kick somewhere else, we collapse. I got kicked in an emotional weak spot that was causing a mental collapse. The problem was that I couldn't seem to get away from the kicks, no matter how hard I tried. It was a part of my life I would need to accept since it wasn't going to change.

Why was I so depressed? Horribly painful feelings from my childhood were surfacing because of issues that were going on in my family. The one I grew up in, not the one with Scott and the kids. Just like in the past when I couldn't connect the food to feelings. Once I could identify them I still couldn't stop the eating. Well, now I couldn't stop the feelings.

I went about my days, functioned normally, and took care of the details of life. My kids were a constant source of joy to me, and when it came to them I could rise above my own personal misery. Scott was extremely supportive, but of course this wasn't his problem. I felt so alone, like some alien, living on Planet Fear.

Of course my eating reflected the pain. Of course my body image was off and it had been for weeks. I canceled plans, stayed out of the circle, and wore big flannel pants every day. My friend Dede threatened to burn them. Especially the blue and green plaid ones with the broken drawstring that dangled on one side. The gray sweatshirt she hated, too, but I would reverse it sometimes for variety; the fleece inside was lighter. I wore it New Year's Eve.

The weather was cold and gray. We were home for winter break. After 9/11, I had asked the kids if they would agree to cancel our upcoming trip and donate the money instead. They agreed right away and I felt so proud of them. I never heard a word of complaint. I was happy in my house. Happy and grateful to be safe. I felt cozy and secure with my family; I just felt low on strength and life.

My physical strength was on a break. Structure was out of town. My trainer had been fired from the gym I had joined and I wasn't working out. Taking care of myself was out the window and I think I developed mothballs. I decided to try something I had heard about, a different sort of training. Core training, it was called. This guy was supposed to be good.

I arrived in my flannel pants to cover up this body I hated. After years of feeling so good and strong, I felt awful to be back in this place. You're probably thinking my weight had changed significantly. It hadn't. Three or four pounds on the scale at that time felt like twenty pounds in my head.

The guy who owned the gym was not a big muscle hound, but he was strong and in perfect shape. He had quite a reputation and lectured all over the world with his training videos and manuals. "Functional training," he explained, takes normal, everyday life movements and combines them with balance and weights.

I was so impressed with his knowledge. His own shape was testimony to his claims. Every movement, every exercise, every routine and circuit, was unique and full of challenge. I learned that my core was the center of my body, the area of my stomach. He taught me to be aware of my core as the origin of all of my strength, and the home base of all of my movement. Everything we did was with a focus on tall posture. Sit-ups would now be a part of my past, but my stomach muscles would be stronger than ever.

His whole theory was "getting some help from your friends." That meant that the muscle being worked drew strength from the other muscles around it. From the very first day we started, he used platforms, balls, and boards to create imbalance. While balancing my body, drawing strength from my core, I would take weights and do repetitions. Often it required balancing on one leg, shifting, and changing direction. Every part of me worked to perform the function. It was a thrill to complete each task. The challenge wasn't lifting the weight. The challenge was maintaining my balance, keeping good form, and always feeling my core.

With each hour session, and I was going twice a week, I felt myself improving. The moves were hard, but so much fun. I loved identifying which muscles were working in a routine; it was always a surprise to see how many different ones came in for the job. This was a welcome change from the pain and monotony of typical weight lifting, which serves no functional purpose. There was something else I was getting here, a message to my emotional side. Core. Balance. Strength. It didn't apply just to my body. It applied to my spirit as well.

I saw it all coming together. My physical body kicked in to "help out its friend," my emotions. My body was teaching my mind to stand tall and find balance in uneven conditions. I was getting a life-changing message. When things in life start to challenge your balance, find the strength within your core.

I noticed that when I lost my focus, I often lost my balance. When I regained the focus, my body performed like magic. The connection was a high. My body was becoming so strong and I was so amazed at its ability to perform.

The slump began to lift. My eating returned to some structure. The pain seemed lighter, an acceptance kicked in, and I began to enjoy life again. Spring had finally arrived. Nothing had changed in my life. The painful parts were certainly there, but they seemed to become somewhat smaller. I kept my focus on the positive things in my life. Looking anywhere else ruined my balance.

In all the years preceding this time, I had learned not to eat from feelings. I had learned to act on them, making changes or choices where needed. What I now had to learn was that feeling something doesn't always call for a change or an action. Sometimes you simply must feel what it is, accept its existence, and find a place to put it. I needed to finally sign at the bottom and approve my life as it was.

I found an answer in the strangest place, having nothing to do with emotions. It had to do with energy, balance, and core. Once again, like Annie Sullivan spelling into Helen's hands, I read from signs that were being spelled in my days, connecting life to spirit. S-T-R-E-N-G-T-H. Once again my world would open.

Chapter 30

Who stole chapter 29? I woke up at four-thirty in the morning and sat down to tell you all sorts of things that were keeping me awake. When I looked for it today it was gone. Son of a bitch! I hate these computers. I've decided that in honor of the missing chapter 29, I'm going straight to chapter 30 and leaving that space open for the day it comes crawling back. It was a beefy chapter, some of those middle-of-the-night thoughts that don't keep middle-of-the-day hours. Oh, well. One of my best friends' husband said he'd pay to read my journals, some that I've been writing for years. If chapter 29 ever comes back, maybe I'll sell it to Norm.

As these pages accumulate, I feel something quite unexpected. I feel a connection to the written words, and to you, my nameless friend. I feel like going to this place in many moments of my day. I feel a sense of purpose I have never felt before. And, like any relationship in the beginning, I find myself wondering where this one will lead me.

There is a comfort I feel with you, but I don't feel that way with others. The other night I was at a restaurant and I watched different women walk in. Some of them looked kind of snooty. I thought to myself, What would it feel like if they read these pages? What if

I heard them whispering about me, "Ooh, she's the one who eats hairy bagels." I guess I'll just need to stand tall.

Journaling is a wonderful release. When you write your feelings to someone, it feels like you're being heard. If the person you write to is someone else, you might anticipate how they'll read it. If the person you write to is yourself, it still feels good to talk. You can get lost in the conversation and you don't have to hear about anyone else. That kind of selfishness is acceptable only in very contained, private places. Therapy and journals are the only ones I can think of, with the rare exception of a special friend who just allows you to vent.

I feel like I'm at summer camp building relationships with new friends. The more time we spend together, the closer I feel to you. I already anticipate the last day of camp, when we will have to go home. Can't you see us hugging in our baseball hats and smell the fumes from the bus? I don't want to think about that now. There's still lots more time together and so much more to share. But when that day arrives, I suggest you make sure you're on my bus. I always pack the best food.

Chapter 31

FLASH BULLETIN: *You are not an irrational person.* But you are when it comes to food. There is a reason you are irrational here, but it has nothing to do with eating. If you were being your rational self, you would be able to see that clearly. You know why you can't? Come on, you can answer that question. When in life are we not able to see things rationally? When we're emotional! We can't always be rational when it comes to our own emotions. When we can't see beyond our own fear.

Typically, when I went in for more tune-ups with Melinda, the same pattern went on in our sessions. Only the names had changed. I used to go in and talk about bagels, cereal, and cookies. Fix that and then I'll be happy. Now I went in with situations. Fix *that* and then I'll be happy.

After these sessions I was cocky and cured. I was way beyond food, emotional wizard that I was now. How amazing it was that the food issues were gone and I could talk about my life. Here's the situation, I'd say, and I'd bat it around like the food. How to work this, how to work that, why couldn't I handle this? Why were my feelings so out of control?

Here's a light example. Just so you know, in emotional calories this was just a snack. But it lets me make a point. Being away from home has always been difficult for me. I obsess about the hotel room; it needs to be cheery. I have a terrible fear of the airplane; I know it's going to crash. I never want to travel without my kids because I don't want them motherless. I don't even like traveling with them because I am terrified of flying.

What if there's a layover and we get stuck at the airport? What if the weather is bad and we circle in the air? What if I die and never come home; who will fix my pillows? Who will make sure they're put in the order that makes them look perfect and poofed?

I could try to distract myself with other thoughts and take the edge off my anxiety. This would be no different than what I used to do when I planned strategies around food. Is this any different than letting the scale determine how I would feel? Why should it matter where I am? Why should it matter what I eat? It doesn't. Both are irrational fears. So where are they coming from?

Melinda would try to go deeper with me, but often there wasn't much time. I was so focused on the situation, just like I focused on the food, that it left little time in the session to cover anything else. The situations would run the gamut from traveling to my marriage. Just like the gamut used to run from restaurants to food on Sundays. What would I do if this was served? . . .

See where I'm going here? Fears of food mimic fears in your life. So what do situational fears mimic? Aha! My fear of travel and airplanes comes directly from my past. When I was a kid I was like a cat; I planted myself in my home. That was safety to me. Any deviation from the structure of home made me anxious and sick to my stomach. When my mom left to go anywhere, I didn't know how to survive it. My fear when she left was primal. What if she never comes back?

My mom went to Spain with Charles for two weeks shortly after they got married. I cried and pleaded with her not to go. After she left, I had a sick feeling in the pit of my stomach. I was alone with my sister. Perhaps I was eleven or twelve. Laurie would play Simon and Garfunkel, and I heard the song "Homeward Bound." I still can't listen to that song today. The feeling of dread, despair, and missing my mom is still so deep inside of me.

Travel triggers that feeling in me. Travel triggers that fear. The fear I had when I was little of being left alone, and being without my mom. Understanding my fear of travel lets me focus in the right place. It lets me see that I have a spot here that I need to be careful with. I need to separate the fearful child from the responsible adult I've become. I need to sit with those feelings. Only then will I be able to move past the fear, in recognition of where it began.

Maybe it means listening to that song. Maybe it means crying for that little girl who felt so alone and abandoned. Maybe it helps to see she survived it and now has kids of her own. Children she kisses and holds every day, making them feel safe with her love.

Now when we're on an airplane, I hold their hands when we take off. Somehow I feel comforted, and they think I'm just cuddling. Don't tell them.

Chapter 32

He was old. He was ugly. He had stubbles on his face. He came around every Saturday and he came with his grown son Joe. Laurie and I would watch through the window as they came to mow our lawn. I was about five years old.

I would walk outside while they were there. I remember when Clarence walked up to me and stooped down to talk to me. I can't tell you how my heart races now, writing this for you to see. I am not sure which is harder, writing it or knowing you'll read it. We were in the backyard behind the house and he knelt in front of me. I will never forget the image.

"Mommy, Clarence tickles my bottom." She looked at my grandfather and he looked back at her. "What do you mean, he tickles your bottom?" she said. "I mean, he tickles my bottom." Bottom to me was the part of my body that was in my underpants.

That was the only conversation. No more questions were ever asked and Clarence kept cutting our lawn. I think it happened again. But, then again, I'm not sure. My memory is of that one place in the yard, in the shadow of our house. Did this lead to problems with food? The honest answer is I don't know. It certainly led to other problems with attitudes toward sex and closeness.

For me sex was dirty and yucky, kind of how Clarence looked. The only thing that could clean it up was being in love with the person. I needed a connection built from words and emotions, not from physical drives. Passion that came from love and commitment was perfectly fine and I loved it. From anywhere else, hang it up.

That "hang it up" attitude is tough on a husband and a marriage. That "hang it up" attitude leaves no room for sex just for fun. That "hang it up" attitude means I am a victim of my past. Well, I don't want to be a victim of my past anymore. I want to have sex 'cause it feels good. Yucky-poo, that's really hard to write! Yucky, yucky, yucky! Spit, spit, petuwie. SpellCheck doesn't recognize *petuwie*. But after sex without closeness, I did! I wanted to rid myself of those words. I wanted to rid my life of those feelings.

I worked through this very slowly with Melinda. I worked through it by allowing it time. I worked through it by having no expectation of myself. And I had a supportive partner. What husband wouldn't want his wife to work on having sex with him? There was no deductible here; I could spend all the money I needed to! Sex just for fun? What an interesting, terrifying concept for me. But Scott knew not to pressure me here; the backlash in that would be huge.

It wasn't that I couldn't have sex. I could. It was just that I couldn't have sex without the emotional closeness, and it had to be really close, in order not to have yuckies. Well, we've spent a lot of time not so emotionally close; that's typical in a marriage. What is not typical is the repulsion I felt when it came just from physical urges, having nothing to do with emotions.

Hey, I know that people don't always want to be with their spouses. I know people who *never* want to be with their spouses! But if they were, it wouldn't be so horrible that they couldn't go on with their day. Without eating cabinets of food. Whoa. I just had a *whoa*. Maybe I'm not so alone! Anybody wish to come forward? Chicken shit!

By golly (*By golly?* Who ever says "By golly"?), is that another secret that none of us is willing to share? Could we fill a million stadiums and all just scream out "YUCK!!"? Do you think we could get SpellCheck to recognize *petuwie*? Really, though, I wanted to know, why couldn't I have sex for sex? Why did it have to be yucky?

This was not about my relationship with Scott. I didn't do this for him. I did this because I spent years held hostage by issues from my past. I wanted to be free of them and be able to make decisions from me the adult, not me the violated child. I wanted to be able to say to him, "I'm in the mood for sex." Without feeling the ghost of my past, and seeing his stubbly face.

How did I do it? To start, I made sure I didn't. I never forced myself or talked myself into having sex just to please my husband. This direction had come straight from our marriage counselor many years ago. "If you don't want to, don't," he said. That was a huge relief, since I knew that if I did, it put me in a terrible place and made me repulsed the next day. I could have saved 16,735,000 calories if I had been told that before. Okay, so maybe that's underestimating; I'd be embarrassed to say the real number.

For Scott, it's not like we were in the best point of our marriage, so he wasn't missing anything he would have been getting anyway. In our past, if we were in a bad place, he didn't have a prayer. At least here he had a trace of one.

It felt like going into really cold water little steps at a time. Sometimes it felt impossible and I walked back onto the sand. Other times I would stand with my ankles covered until I got used to it. Sometimes I would just stay away from the water and not even consider it. Other times something motivated me and I just jumped in without caution.

It wasn't the "during" that was the problem. It was the after part. It was the deep disappointment that I felt this way. It was the devastating chants I would say to myself: "Why do I have to feel this?" It was like the chants I used to say in the mirror after I ate tons of food: "I hate myself!" It wasn't that I hated myself; what I hated was how I felt.

I was also lucky to have a husband who was patient with my issues. He never put pressure on me since he knew where the difficulty came from. One place it came from was his lack of emoting, which was so difficult for me, given these issues I had. I know he appreciated how hard I worked to overcome that. And to be honest, I felt like I owed him for putting up with all of my bullshit. Have I mentioned that I can be quite a handful?

With time, with repetition, with a willingness to feel that discomfort, and to share these feelings with Scott, amazingly it happened.

The yuckies slowly diminished. Something I used to be so terribly afraid of is something I now can enjoy.

I have read that many people with eating disorders have had incidents of a sexual nature somewhere in their past. Perhaps the severity of our response with food stems from that place of betrayal. Someone fucked with our boundaries. No wonder we're so confused.

Things like that weren't supposed to happen; that's why no one listened. As a little girl I had done the right thing, I had gone to the people I trusted. I can't blame my mom for what she didn't know, but I have made a vow to myself. Never again will that girl inside me be ignored when she's calling for help. I will always promise to listen to her. That's why I don't need the food.

And I have a husband who actually gets some! A trace of a prayer came through.

Chapter 33

"*Oh, my gosh, I could never do that. What would people think?*"

People with eating issues often have trouble with the judgment of others. We invest so heavily in what people think of us and we want everyone to like us. We look for validation in much of what we do. We avoid situations that might make us the target of criticism or disapproval. And then we get it anyway.

I took a volunteer position overseeing the day camp in the town where we spend our summers. I had three kids in the camp and it was a nice way to give back to the community. I was close with the counselors and the kids who came to camp and I felt a satisfaction in knowing that my presence made a difference.

The director ran the camp every day, and we got along beautifully. Those of us inside the camp knew that the camp was what it was, a simple, no-frills, run-by-the-seat-of-its-pants kind of place. There wasn't the money or manpower to make it much more than that.

In the winter before my third summer in this position, I told the board that ran the camp, of which I was a member, that I felt it would be best if I stepped down. We were moving in June and I knew my time out there would be more fragmented. I was asked to stay because there was no one else to fill the position and I was assured that whatever time I spent there would be fine. I reluctantly agreed to stay on.

Ironically, to compensate for what I thought would be less time, I actually spent the most time ever there. It was my strongest summer yet. I'd wake up at five-thirty in the morning sometimes to drive in from the city, just to make breakfast for the counselors. I knew that the more energy I gave to them, the more they would give to the campers.

I implemented an art fair to display the campers' artwork. I wrote skits for the talent show, improved our relations with the village office, pulled a quitting art director back in, and made runs to the store when we ran low on supplies unexpectedly. I spent my mornings there, rather than relaxing at home or exercising with the other moms while all of our kids were at camp.

I told the board I would be gone for four days; I needed to deal with workmen at my home in the city. No big deal. No big deal until lots and lots of tiny lice decided to find homes in the hair of our campers. It was an epidemic. Panic, pandemonium, and lots of upset parents. Some of the parents and other members of the board came in to help out. Everything was handled beautifully in my absence.

Icy. Not the Popsicles, the people. I came back to lots of disapproval. No comments or kudos for what I had done had ever come my way in my three years on the job. But now I was getting some feedback. Where in the world was I? And, by the way, I later heard they didn't like how I dressed. I wore cropped tops and my stomach showed, not appropriate attire for a camp. Hey, now. Literally hit below the belt. I love my belly! I have no chest, so it's kind of all I've got going. What the heck was this?

Criticisms of the day camp were expected. They were a part of the camp's forty-something years' history. The criticism to me personally was harder to hear. Especially hearing it secondhand. I felt terrible about the disapproval. All of the efforts I had made were apparently not worth mentioning. Only the length of my shirt.

The reason I am bringing this up is because I put myself out there with the best of intentions, and got kind of slammed for it in the process. I know it may happen with this book. And it will feel a whole lot worse if it does. This is personal. This book is as intimate as it gets.

Judgment is tough when you know who you are inside and others can see only the outside. I have learned not to judge anyone's behavior because I know there's a story behind it. I spent more than forty years hating my belly. We're finally spending some quality time together. That was my story. So shoot me again.

That is my fear today. It's why I'm feeling jumpy. I am committed to this. I believe in what I have to say and I want to be there for you. But it's going to be very strange to know people can see inside. I'll be an open target and they could nail my inny to the wall. Oh, well. I guess I'll have to belly up.

Chapter 34

"*Wow, how did it get to be noon already!*"

We'll deal with two kinds of lunches here, one for eating at home and one for eating out. If it's eating out and it's a business lunch, we'll deal with that one as well. Let's start at home.

Are you terribly starving? We got involved in talking and our hunger may be bigger than we thought. We'd better slice an apple, or pull out some carrots to munch on while we make our lunch. Otherwise we'll start eating everything else in sight, before we ever sit down. And then we'll get that scary look about us, and I just can't go there right now!

Think about the food in the fridge. Think about the food you could make. Think about what sounds good, and do not, I repeat *do not,* think in terms of what you should have in order to lose weight. You will lose weight. But right now our focus is lunch. Don't look ahead; it will mess you up. Put your attention to this meal. This is lunchtime. You are hungry. This is your green light to eat.

What sounds good? Are you in the mood for something with bread, like a sandwich? Do you want to try a Boca burger with some ketchup and melted low-fat cheese along with lettuce and tomato? Do you want a salad because it feels light and kind of healthy? That's just fine, but make sure you add either protein, like turkey, or some kind of bread alongside it; otherwise it won't be enough. Don't overdo the dressing, and remember the suggestions on pages 127–128.

You could make your own egg-white omelet. Try whipping six whites with a blender or electric mixer. It will make it fluffy, full, and light. The best is one of those milk-shake machines, the kind you see in a soda fountain. They whip them just to a froth.

Take a frying pan, and sauté some mushrooms, onions, or other vegetables you like in some cooking spray. You don't need to use that much. Pour in your frothy egg whites. Scramble or make it an omelet and try adding low-fat cheese. Tomatoes are good in there, too. If you don't add cheese, have some toast. Or maybe half of a bagel with some light cream cheese.

What do you need to end your meal? Something sweet? Have one of those calcium chews. Or have a small piece of candy. If you feel safe, have yourself one or two cookies. Whatever you decide feels right is exactly what you should have. Make this meal structured. It has a beginning and an end. Plates are good things; use them. Don't stand and eat at the counter. Sit like a person and eat.

What about my friends at work? Is it hard to go out to a restaurant and not overeat? Do you find yourself feeling safer with food when you eat alone in the office? When you're on a diet, does bringing your own food make it easier? Let's figure out the answers.

Examine which days are the hardest with food. Examine which restaurant, which people you go with, and what days of the week are the worst. Let's say that there are some clients or business associates you have to meet. And let's say that in anticipation of meeting them, all you see is that basket of bread. You know this will be hard and you wish you could get out of going. But you can't.

Let's walk through some possibilities of what's really going on here. After all, when you walk down the street and see bakeries, do they make you anxious and nervous? If they're not a problem and the bread basket is, let's look at who's at that table. Besides Mr. Sour Dough and Ms. Crusty Millet.

Perhaps you don't like these people. Perhaps they bore the shit out of you. Or maybe you feel nervous around them because they could influence your business. Maybe doing business around food is the worst thing we could do. Conducting business is complicated enough. You need to be on, you need to think, and there is an element of pressure. For someone with eating issues of any kind, this is a runaway train.

So, let's consider the choices here. Number one, if you don't like the people and you can get out of it, get out of it. Don't go if you would rather not go. You have that right to say no, especially if this is social. Number two, if this is a business lunch, does it have to be done over lunch? Is there a way to make an appointment that does not take place in a restaurant? Can it be held in someone's office instead? If the answer is no, let's deal with *that* loaded gun. Here's what you need to do.

Establish your discomfort and where it comes from by examining the person or people you're meeting. Think through your relationship, lack of relationship, or overall opinion of them. Once you pinpoint where your discomfort or dislike is, feel it before you go. Admit to yourself how much you dread this and how hard it is to be there. It's hard to spend time where you don't want to be, with people you don't want to be with.

You need to take care of yourself here. You need to listen to your feelings. You need to allow yourself to be the child who screams, *"I don't want to go to that lunch!"* Then you need to be the caretaker who says, "I know, but we have to go anyway. There are some things in life we don't want to do but we need to just get through them." The child feels bad, whines for a while, and goes along in tow. That's what you'll have to do here, after the child in you sulks a bit.

Acknowledging those feelings *before* the lunch will prepare you for what lies ahead. Someone you don't want to be with. Some business that causes you stress. Look at it this way. Eating from the bread basket makes you feel better for a moment, but when you finish scarfing it down, guess who's still sitting there? The same person you didn't want to sit with *before* you ate the bread!

If you know the restaurant, preplan what you'll eat. Make decisions before you get there and stick to them as you order. If you decide to allow some bread, then have exactly what you planned. If it feels safer to stay away from the bread, then stay away from the bread.

If you do not know the menu, make a decision that feels healthy and light to you. You wouldn't want to go unhealthy or heavy; it will throw off your sense of control. A salad with some chicken, dressing on the side. Chicken, fish, or a turkey something; maybe a bowl of soup. You may want to stay away from pasta and sauces or things that are heavy and rich.

Remember, it's not the food you can't control, it's that awful feeling. You cannot control the way you feel, but you *can* control what you eat. One more word of caution. You may make it through the lunch. You may feel very relieved at the great job you did. But you are still on high alert. It took a great deal of energy to hold back from overeating in light of what you were feeling. Once you relax back into your day, that food energy may surface again. You need to watch out and here's how.

Make sure there is something in the office to eat late in the afternoon. Don't leave yourself foodless. Don't go home starving either. You just did something difficult and you are an emotional person. What if some grateful client brings you banana bread? Oozing with chocolate chips? You might devour it all without thinking.

Have something around to curb your hunger that also tastes good to you. Zone Perfect bars are the perfect afternoon snack; make sure you keep some around. Always have an apple with you, too. I don't recommend chips or pretzels as an afternoon snack unless they're accompanied by something else. They won't fill you up, and in times of trouble they can catapult you into a binge. That's why I like the bars. They are filling, satisfying, and packaged in one serving. I believe they are the safest snack. Make sure you drink water as well.

No one said this was easy! Not in a world where children come home with candy from a party at school. Not when coworkers come in with Girl Scout cookies. Who can pass up Thin Mints? Have a great lunch. Have a midafternoon snack. It keeps a chain on the door of your hunger, and those big, bad binges can't get in.

Chapter 35

"*I feel too fat to go!*"

Guess what I figured out? A binge is just an excuse. An excuse not to go to a party, an excuse not to go out with friends, an excuse not to go to the gym and even not to go to work. And dare I say it? An excuse not to have sex tonight. How many times have you eaten too much just before doing something that you really don't want to do? How about this crazy idea? Don't do it. Don't go to the party, don't meet the friend, and don't have sex when you don't want to. *Say no without the food.* Make the choice without the force. Simply make the choice.

Sometimes I used to feel a burning energy; something had me running inside. As I stuffed the food into my mouth, I'd think about needing to exercise it off. Maybe the bingeing in that very moment was the need to run off steam. Do I need to eat the food to justify the run? Do I need to pack on calories to have the excuse to burn them off? What I really need to do is run out the door and *run*. Or walk out the door and walk *fast*.

Last night I had that energy; I could sense it was jumpy nerves. I knew it was anxiety and a run would have done me some good. I skipped the binge and asked Scott to take a brisk walk with me, so we could talk about all the things that were making me feel so jumpy. I wanted to tell you about that. Physical movement is a healthy way to redirect energy. Don't speed around the block to exercise and don't do it as a distraction. Do it because the feelings are caged and they need to be given a run.

Remember my doggy Snickers? Sometimes he feels caged up even when he's not in a cage. Sometimes that dog needs to run. And it's not because he wants to lose weight. His jeans weren't tight this morning. Imagine exercise just because it feels good and releases energy inside. Jumpy feelings need to jump. Anxiety needs to race. Nervousness needs to sprint. Your body needs to move.

This is not about burning calories, though certainly it does. It's to connect physical and emotional muscles. The ones that kick in to survive. When you're emotions are low, let your physical being wake them. When your physical being is low, use your spirit to liven it up. Create your own inner balance. That's what inflates the life preserver. It's what floats your pain to shore.

Chapter 36

Kids eat the darndest things. Remember that day at the restaurant? When I ordered what I was led to believe was a chicken sandwich, not a bite in a bun? I didn't tell you what my brilliant five-year-old did.

He ordered a cheeseburger and finished it. He was still hungry, so he asked us to order another one. *Another one?* Yes, he insisted he really wanted more. So while I ate everyone's fries, chips, and parts of my chair, he ate another burger. Stupid! I should have just ordered more food. I should have done what he did. A whole other sandwich would have probably been equal to less than half of what I ended up eating instead. Kids are smart. They have a natural sense of what they need. Until food issues mess with their instincts.

Many of us grew up with a tremendous pressure to be thin. Often if we weren't battling our own weight, we lived with someone who did. The problems that kids have today with food are worse than ever before. Eating disorders and obesity are rampant in our country. There are organizations and facilities to help both kids and adults deal with these problems. But I believe they sometimes chase people away by telling them what they can't hear. I visited a chapter of one of the larger organizations recently and I was disturbed by what I saw.

I observed one of their support groups, held in a hospital. The format is to go around the room, talk about your week, discuss events in your life, and say whatever comes to mind. You are not allowed to talk about food. You cannot discuss your "behaviors," meaning your means of control. I understand the philosophy behind that rule; get away from the obsession and talk about the issues behind it. The point is valid and right. But it's not the only point.

There is a connection that takes place in a support group. It lets each person know that he or she isn't alone. But when it comes to food, people are taught that any form of calorie concern is *that* behavior." And I don't agree with that view.

What struck me was when one of the girls in the group explained that on this particular day, she had eaten lightly and healthfully and felt pretty good about that. She then wondered if that was good or bad. She wondered if her healthy eating was returning to "negative behaviors." I felt so sad for her confusion. And angry that she got no answer. She was questioning her own decisions, ones that felt good on that day. Because her concern was food-related, she was not encouraged to discuss it. I was simply outraged.

Had I walked into Melinda's office and been instructed not to discuss food, I wouldn't have stuck with my therapy. I needed to talk about food and I needed to talk about my life. I needed to learn to live with both, since I had to face both every day.

My discussions of food, meals, shopping tips, and planning are an attempt to teach you how to make smart and knowing choices. My talk of exercise has not been about weight control at all. It's been to connect you with your strength. I do not at all support a skinny look, one that's achieved by incessant dieting. But I do support you at your very best. Optimal health, energy, and spirit.

I would be doing you a disservice if I told you simply to respect yourself and stay away from food-obsessing. Or directed you to a nutritionist who will teach you the right food groups without asking you where you feel safe. Or to therapists who deal only with the emotional side; do they help you understand how to deal with the world of food? That world that holds all your fears?

The leader of this support group was overweight. While I don't make it my business to judge anyone's decision about their own weight, I do know that being overweight is not considered optimal for health. I don't happen to think it's any healthier than being underweight.

And let's face it. If we want to lose weight and be healthy, who are we going to seek help from? Someone who is overweight and believes that's acceptable? Would I have trusted Melinda had she been twenty pounds heavier and said it was okay if I was? Not in a million years.

The way to frighten any young person or adult with food obsessions is to tell them it's okay to be overweight. They'll run. Literally. They will run miles and miles to make sure that doesn't happen to them. Conversely, the worst way to deal with obesity in kids and adults is to set up rules and restrictions. It will lead only to sneaking food and bingeing privately.

Again, I'm only one rat. I ran one maze. But I got out. I am not suggesting that you eat what I eat or believe what I believe. I can't know what's best for you. All I am trying to do is encourage you to find that out for yourself. I think it's healthy to watch what you eat. I think it's healthy to eat some junk. I think it's unrealistic to discourage the mention of food and eating. Everyone talks about food. Why should those with problems be left out of that conversation?

You want to be overweight? That is certainly your choice. You want to weigh less? We can get you there as well. Is it eating-disorder behavior to want to be thin? No, I think it's a wonderful goal so long as it's achieved with comfort, without governing your life, and with the utmost concern for good health. And spiritual health as well.

I'm trying to make you feel safe. Not safe in being underweight. Not safe in being overweight. Safe in knowing that all of your choices will ultimately be your own. Just as they are today. Can I make that choice for you now? Can your parent, your spouse, your coach, your boyfriend, your girlfriend, or your doctor tell you what they think you should do? Well, sure they can. And you'll do exactly what you do now. You'll listen to them, you'll respond or you won't, and in private you'll do what you want to do.

Listen to everyone. And then make your own decisions, based on what's best for you. You have a voice, and all I wish for you is to find out what's underneath the importance you place upon food, and what's underneath your fear of it. Why is it so hard to have comfort and ease in this portion of your life?

Don't say it's because you love food. You should love food. Don't say it's because you really don't like food and it makes you feel sick to eat it. There is nothing sickening about food. Search to find your answers.

When a child is afraid of the dark, we don't close the door to make it darker and tell her not to be fearful. We find a way to comfort her, and offer her what makes her feel safe. We let her sleep with a night-light on. Eventually, as she gets older and feels safer in her world, she learns to sleep in the dark. Eventually, as you feel safe with your feelings, you will begin to feel safe with food, and won't be so afraid.

It's okay to be thin. Sleep tonight with that light on. It is healthy to be at a good weight. You are not wrong to want that in your life. It is not okay to starve, purge, binge, or exercise to exhaustion. It is not okay to jump from diet to diet and put so much energy there. The scary monsters there are just feelings inside of you.

If you are someone who throws up food, what you really need is to throw up your feelings. If you are someone who tries not to eat at all, what you're trying to do is not *feel*. Once you let those feelings come out and be heard, food won't scare you anymore.

The funny thing about monsters in the closet and scary feelings inside is that what makes them so scary is just that they're hidden and we're not sure when they'll jump out. Sitting face-to-face with feelings is really not so bad. They can be a little bit ugly. But they have fascinating features. When you find out where they come from it's always quite a story. In literature it's called a fable. In life it's called your story. And what a page-turner you'll turn out to be.

Chapter 37

Photo albums are full of pictures that look perfect. We pose, we smile, we suck in our gut, and we flip our hair just right. We make sure there's nothing in our teeth and we make our faces look happy. We don't just do it in pictures, do we? We do it in our lives, every single day. But what's behind that perfection? If we were to take a picture inside our lives, what would that picture show?

An obsession of any kind reflects something else underneath. Rarely do we show it. It's hidden behind the pose. We become consumed in the obsession privately. We blame it for messing up our lives. We hold it responsible for what we don't have. But the real reason for our unhappiness is something else altogether. We don't want to face the truth because *that* would mess up our lives. An obsession is safer to blame.

If the obsession is food, alcohol, drugs, sex, shopping, a person, gambling, money, or frog collecting, behind it is a feeling. The obsession takes over. We are drawn to it and we can't stay away. The distraction may feel good and pleasurable. Or it may feel horrible. Either way, after we have engaged in it, we feel a terrible crash. What's in the crash? The feeling of "not enough" or the feeling of needing more?

Not thin enough, but needing more food to feel better. Not

enough of a buzz; needing another drink. There's always more shopping to do; spending money makes us feel better. Another procedure done to make us feel better about our looks. What's the message behind it all?

The next time you obsess about another person, call your own bluff. If you think someone else has it better just because they're thin, rich, successful, smart, or whatever, figure out what you think they have. Happiness? That they're good enough? Is that what they have over you? What did thin bring them that you want? Do you think they are more loved and admired? Now take away their thin. What's left? What do they have that you want?

Take your focus off them. Take your focus off thin. Put that focus on yourself and face the truth for once. Get ready because it's going to hurt. Come on, what is it? What's behind that obsessing? Who didn't love you enough? Who told you that you weren't good enough? It wasn't you, it was someone else. We're not born thinking we need to be better. Stay with me here.

When was the last time you were good enough? When you were five? When you were ten? Before some event in your life? When did you become so unworthy? Were you fine until something happened? What was the something that happened?

The obsession pulls us in and we can't stop it. We are so angry at ourselves. We regressed again. We feel low, weak, and defeated. Each time we go back we feel worse, and further and further away. It's like crawling into a hole, and that's a lonely place to be. It's a place to go into hiding so that no one sees us.

It's not the food and it's not your stomach hanging over your belt. It's your dark side. A dark side is not a bad thing; a dark side is a real thing. It's you in the raw. It may be volatile, wild, and full of rage. Bottled-up feelings and experiences that you corked long ago want out. You want to keep them in. The obsession is the cork, don't you see? You let go of that and it's like exploding champagne, without the celebration.

Someone or something shook your insides and that's why you have these obsessions. Until you let out the feelings from that, the obsessions will stay with you. We need to get you to pop the cork and let those feelings come out. Let me tell you what that did for me.

When I have let go of my feelings, the horribly painful ones, it *does* feel like throwing up, but I am not talking about food. I mean deep, wrenching sobs that come from my gut, and don't stop until my gut feels empty. Feelings can make us feel that kind of sick. And just like throwing up, which you do *not* want to do, getting the feelings out will make you feel better.

Once Scott and I were with our marriage counselor. I was telling the counselor about feelings from my past that were very hard to discuss. He asked me some questions and I told him thinking about it made me feel queasy and sick. He pointed to the garbage can and said, "Maybe that's what you need. Maybe you need to throw up." I've never been a thrower-upper. But it made me understand people who are. It's not to get rid of the food, as they think it is. It's an attempt to get rid of the feelings.

There may be feelings inside you that are making you sick. So come on. Let it out. Find someone's arms to cry in, or hold this book to your chest. Know that I am here with you and I have been in that kind of pain. Look at me, I'm still standing. I got through it and so will you. Come on now, my friend. It's time to just let it go.

Chapter 38

There is nothing like a good girlfriend. The kind who knows every part of you and loves you like a sister. The kind who stands up for you and protects you like a mom. The kind who makes you so comfortable that you'd rather talk than eat. I hate to sound judgmental, but some friends make me hungry. And other friends make me feel full.

Many people with food issues won't confide in a friend. I will tell you that finding someone and trusting him or her will dramatically change your life. Most of us have been burned at one time or another by someone who betrayed us. When I choose who I confide in, I am extremely careful. How do we know who to trust? Here are some points to consider.

Is this person warm and kind? Is she someone you respect? Is she betraying other peoples' confidences? She may betray yours as well. Does she talk only about herself? How does she treat other people? Is she consistent and dependable? I don't mean in her actions. I mean in her heart and intent.

And finally, trust your instincts. Look at your level of comfort. Be careful, though; while this works most of the time it's not always foolproof. Sometimes people are uncomfortable initially, because it takes them time to warm up. Or maybe it clicks right away, but fizzles out after a while. Let it evolve over time. Remember how we started out before we got comfortable? Now our trust is unbreakable. It will be the same when you step off the page.

When you reveal your innermost secrets, and secrets are revealed back to you, there's a trust and connection so deep and strong that you will actually feel a high. The secret may be one that makes you feel sad, but the friend helps you feel good again. The friend makes you feel loved and accepted, no matter what she hears.

Then again, some friends are really there when things are going badly for you, but when you're in a good place, they aren't quite as supportive. Envy gets in the way of the good friend they want to be. I don't judge them anymore, but I will tell you this. The biggest challenge any friend faces is to share in another friend's joy. Especially when that very happiness is something they feel deprived of.

Many years ago, my friend Sheila moved into a magnificent home. Scott and I had very little money then. I wondered what it would feel like to live in such a big house. I found myself obsessing about it and I hated how that felt. I would hold back my enthusiasm and act like it didn't impress me. But the envy ate at my insides. You know how I got over it? I told her I wanted her house. I asked her what it felt like to live in such a beautiful place. Did it get me over the jealousy? Hell, no! But at least it didn't feel ugly.

I found that competitions never exist in the deeper friendships. You never hold back a compliment if the friendship is pure. You may feel jealous. You may look at her and want what she has. Telling people you envy them relieves the bad feeling inside. Instead of feeling a twinge of resentment, you feel like a giving friend. You go on and on stroking her ego. If she's a good friend, she deserves that.

Here's one I'll bet you're familiar with. Have you ever known someone who wants you to eat fattening foods and encourages you to overeat them? My friend Dede does the opposite. If she thinks I'm overeating, she immediately moves the food away. I take that the right way. I used to have a friend who moved food close to me after I had pushed it away. Knowing my history, Dede is protecting me. She won't ever let me put myself down. She has a wicked sense of humor, and when I'm low I know she will lift me.

Whenever I used to have lunch with my friend April, it was hard to get past her beauty. I felt like a frump around her. So I just came out and told her. "I feel like a cow around you!" That was when we got close. She told me what she felt insecure about. She said what she admired in me. We bonded on the insecurities that each of us had.

Now when we meet for lunch, I swear it's as though the world just stops. I know that sounds melodramatic, but that's exactly what it feels like to us. It feels like the ultimate love fest. If a cell phone rings, let them call back, we are too engrossed in each other. When the food comes to the table, our mouths don't have time for it. Since we don't get together often, we can't trade in words for bites.

When it comes to my closest friends, we all have complicated personalities and we're all honest about it. We know it's our greatest asset and we know it's our greatest curse. When we're up it's like we're supercharged and ready to lasso the world. When we're down we feel low on energy and it feels like the battery's dead. A good girlfriend is always there, with a set of jumper cables.

My friend Ruthie is brilliant, logical, energetic, and extremely successful in her career. She is a single mom with a high-powered job. She juggles her life beautifully. I have always been so impressed with her and her financial independence, since the only way I ever earned money was to buy something and return it!

One night a couple of years ago, Ruthie and I were out to dinner. I was telling her about all of my stuff at the time, all of the complicated issues I had and how I couldn't resolve them. I always trust her opinion and she understands me so well. This night, however, she looked completely exhausted from me. She combed through her gorgeous thick hair with her hand, and gave me some sound advice. "Nancy, you need a job."

Each of my friends plays a vital role in my life and I play a vital role in theirs. We are able to give each other a perspective that we are too emotional to see in ourselves. A best friend can listen and understand but challenge you at the same time. Ruthie was right. Obsessing about my emotions had become my full-time job. I needed to find a new one.

Because Ruthie was in the professional world, she could see that my energy needed to be refocused and put into something constructive. There was truly no other answer and none of my problems would be resolved at that time. She saw me banging my head against a wall. Now I see that when there isn't an answer, that's when obsessions take over. It's not just to cover a feeling. Obsessing is trying to find a solution where there isn't one to find. Not everything is solvable.

Scott and I have a friend who is dashingly handsome, and has the perfect body and a discipline that surpasses all. We've known him for a very long time. One thing he and I have in common is that we were both chubbers in the past.

He describes himself as simply fine-tuning his body. He knows it's good but says it could always be a little better. He watches his fat grams and calories. He orders pizzas and cancels them. He told me he feels bad about what I have been through with food, but he doesn't have those problems. But I know he does. And this was the day he confirmed it.

He told me I should be proud of what great shape I'm in. He told me he thought I was perfect. I told him he had just described himself. He said, as he pointed to his taut skin, "Well I could lose two more pounds, get rid of this blubber here, and then I would be pretty happy." I looked at him and just stared with my mouth hanging open. Then I asked him, "Will there ever be a point where you'll look at yourself and think you're good enough?" And then he said the most revealing thing. "Oh, no, I certainly hope not. If I ever reached that goal, what would I have to think about?" Whoooah. What would he have to think about? I called him in on that one, big time.

I told him that obsessing about his weight or his looks is no different than obsessing about food or anything else. If you set a goal that can never be met, you need to question the goal. There is nothing wrong with perfecting, and fine-tuning can be a great thing. Reaching a goal is so satisfying, but there's a certain disappointment, too. It means it's over. You got there. Now what?

Using our weight and our bodies as a goal is very safe in one way. We will always have a goal. We will always have a purpose. Since our bodies can never be without flaw, there is always some new goal to find. Without the obsession, without the goal, life would be a total bore.

Because of my history, I think I'll always have issues with food and weight. And I don't suspect they will ever be completely gone. One of the reasons why, though, is that I do place an importance on keeping myself at an "ideal" weight. Is it obsessive? No, but it used to be. Now it's a price I pay to maintain myself in the place where I feel my best. And that is a choice I make.

I don't like the feeling of gaining weight, of my clothes being tight, or of feeling overfull. Does that make me obsessed? I know what obsessed feels like. This feels more like driven. Like maintaining the place I've worked for.

My friend has a very successful business and he is highly regarded in his field. But maybe that professional goal which has been met has become one he knows in and out. Maybe he needs a new goal. Perhaps if he filled whatever the void is, his body would be perfect enough.

Your efforts to be in better shape are commendable. Your inability to give yourself credit is a problem. Was there someone in your past who didn't give you credit, either? You lost a pound? Great! Be your own your own best fan and don't let others determine your cheers.

One other important point: The time or effort it takes to lose weight goes a lot faster with less effort when you're busy. Busy with something of interest, having nothing to do with food. That's why I got me a job now.

Friends and goals soak up voids. It doesn't take a soul mate to make you feel great inside. I have friends who I don't see that often, like my summertime friends in the country, and other friends who go way back. I have buddies in the neighborhood who are always so warm and kind.

When you fill a void with food, you get full and it makes you feel bad. When you fill a void with a friend, you feel full and rich and lucky. Why do you think I wanted you to bypass the chapters with food? I want you to see that when you engage in a person, food becomes second choice. If you weren't all that engaged in me, and you read the food chapters instead, it's quite all right. *Just you wait.* I'll get you in the end, my pretty. And I'll get your little dog, too!

Chapter 39

If you asked me where my dreams got started, my answer would be the car window. As a child and as an adult, my mind would escape the car I was in and jump into someone else's. The dreaming I did as I stared out the window was looking for another life. Beyond the one that I had. Like Dorothy in *The Wizard of Oz*, I dreamed of someplace with color.

When Dorothy woke up from her dream, it took her a moment to separate the dream from the place she lived. The Scarecrow, the Lion, the Tin Man. Finally she was home, back in her bed in Kansas. And then the movie ended.

What we never found out was what life was like in Kansas. We saw the storm lift her home. We saw it land somewhere else. Dorothy wore shoes that would ultimately bring her the very thing she searched for. She just didn't know it at the time. But why had she left in the first place? What was wrong in Kansas?

Maybe she was overeating. Maybe she was obsessing. Maybe she was searching for more. She never ate in Oz, you know. No one ever did. Did anyone ever stop for lunch in the Emerald City? Pack a picnic for the field of poppies? Bring food along for the balloon ride? And what about the good witch, Glinda? What made her sparkle so?

I want a sequel. I want to know what was up with Kansas. I

want to know why the house blew away. Then I want to know what life was like after the house came back. What did the Tin Man, Scarecrow, and Lion do in the dream that was different from when they were home?

And why, oh why, was that dream in color? Why was Kansas black-and-white? It was safe. It was comfortable. It was everything she knew. Did Dorothy ever find color in Kansas, or was it only to be in her dreams?

Fairy tales and fantasies are too good to stay in the books. And their messages are so important if we bring them into our lives. Cinderella has all the answers. She may have gotten all gussied up to meet her prince, but that was just the first date. In the end he found her and loved her for who she was. The other women tried to fit into the slipper, but comfort cannot be forced. When something fits it just does. It is then that the food isn't needed.

My life has not been black-and-white. But writing to you has brought so much more color. My very own land of Oz in the quiet of my own words. You know, Dorothy wasn't the only one who got her wish in the dream. The Lion got his courage. The Tin Man got his heart. The Scarecrow got his brain. And Dorothy got to go home. I guess that leaves hope for us, too.

So, let's click our heels together and repeat those words three times. "There's no place like home. There's no place like home. There's no place like home." That place so deep inside. Where homesick never happens, where sleep is sound, and where dreams really do come true.

Chapter 40

The rat has a friend who's a mouse. She's been my friend since we were fifteen; that's when I named her Mushmouse. She has a house in the country, too, around the corner from mine. Not long ago, we spent the day together. Without actually realizing where we were headed, we found ourselves in a binge. Two little rodents in the kitchen.

It was a Monday. We were watching the kids in her pool. We were both feeling a little frumpy; looks don't matter much out here. Makeup isn't worth putting on, and we don't wash our hair as often as we should either. It just gets dirty again. By the time August comes around we feel like we're growing ivy.

We were feeling just a little bored. All this relaxing can be tiring. I had fifteen people coming for dinner that night, including her and her kids. I hadn't done anything yet, and I wanted to leave and get ready, but she didn't want me to go. Not yet. I told her I was getting stir crazy. We were giggling about how she didn't want me to leave. I begged her. "I know," she said, as she led me to her porch. "Let's sit down and play one hand of cards." "ARE YOU KIDDING ME?" I screamed. "Let me out of here!" Finally, I agreed to stay. But not without her apple pie.

I told her that if she was making me stay, I would have to eat. And I wasn't going there alone. If I was going down, she was going with me. She was far too desperate at this point to refuse any offer I made. We ate a small piece of pie. Probably suspecting that she needed to sustain my stay with more, she pulled out ice cream sandwiches. "Now you're talking," I said, "but let me show you how it's really done." I opened up her pantry. "I'm going to teach you how to binge right."

I pulled out the graham crackers, got out the ice cream, and made her a nice little sandwich. She liked that okay, but she had another idea. She went and retrieved a banana, which was probably the most movement I had seen out of her that day. "See this?" she said, and she put ice cream on the banana. "Too much soft," I said. "I need something crunchy."

Remember I told you never to shop in bulk? Here's why. Inside the pantry was a huge bag of snack-mix stuff, but this one was particularly good. I began to eat out of the bag. Seeing the problem with her own banana, she placed some of it right on top. "That's disgusting," I told her. "No," she insisted, "this is really good."

She may have been feeling the threat of an end, the possibility that at some near moment, I would break down and leave to cook dinner. So she decided to pull out what she considered her very own grand slam. Cora Lee toffees. Devastated she was when she took a bite and knew there was a problem. They were soft. They weren't crunchy like toffee should be. That was it. I was going home to make dinner. "How about if I stick them in the freezer?" She frantically groped for something to pull me back. Poor Mushy had pretty much exhausted her options with me.

I went home to cook dinner. Hadn't had a binge like that in a long, long time. Hadn't done it with a friend since those days back in college with Domino's pizza and Rich 'n Chips. What was going on? And why was it so much fun? And why didn't I hate myself? Why didn't I hate Mushy?

I could have asked her why she knowingly used a weakness of mine just to make me stay. I could have wondered what friend would bring out the food instead of letting me go. I could have judged the moment and made the decision that she didn't care about me. Or she wanted to see me fail. But I know Mushy better than that. And I know how much she loves me. I had to take away my own doubt in her and try to see what had happened.

She needed me. She didn't want to be alone. She was sensing my need to get back to my house but she wanted me to stay longer. It's not like she sat and thought about it or created some strategy. What she saw was that once I started eating I wasn't leaving her. And that was what she needed. To be protective of me by pulling away food would have allowed me to go home. But that would have left her alone.

If she'd been able to say "I need you to stay," or "I'm feeling so anxious right now," we could have taken those extra moments and talked each other through it. The fact that I was bingeing in such quantity meant that I needed something as well. Going home to cook dinner or being bored with the day was not all that was going on. A binge that size speaks of more.

Here we were in our summer retreats, but summer was almost over. We talked about which week we'd head home and how we couldn't believe summer was over. Home means the end of vacation. Home means another transition. Home means heading back to real life; we had been talking about it that morning. The house lands back in Kansas. For Mushy there were things that were stressful to her awaiting her at home. For me as well there was something painful that I soon had to face.

The summer is almost over and the pages are winding down. And this summer you've been my color. It's been the best summer of my life. I've asked you to answer the question, What would life be like without food? Well, I'll have to face a question myself: What will life be like without you?

Just like Mushy, I'm not quite ready for that. Would you mind staying a little bit longer? How about staying for a snack and dinner? I promise to watch out for you.

Chapter 41

Most people I know have a hard time with food in the late afternoon, especially if they are home. This is when kids come home from school. This is when most babies aren't napping. This may be when preparations for dinner are starting up. There are two possibilities if you're focused on food. One is that you are hungry. The other is something else. Let's deal with the hunger first, and talk about good options for snacks.

We need to be careful with food here. As we're learning what these emotions are doing, we need to hold on to structure. Consider that structure your anchor. It holds you in place and keeps you grounded while the waves throw the boat around. It's in this way that a diet can work for you. Not the part about deprivation; you have learned the danger in that. But diets can offer an organized format instead of food that's scattered.

It's late afternoon. It's been a few hours since lunch. It's getting closer to the end of the day. That includes a variety of situations. If you're a mom with young kids, this is the longer part of the day, when they are usually finished with napping. If your kids are older, it's the time they come home from school. Not what we'd call quiet time! If you are at work, you've been there for some time now and you see that the day's almost over. And last, mere transitions can cause us to eat.

Then there is another possibility that many of us don't like to look at. It's possible that during the day you are fine. You are busy, occupied, and surrounded by details that put food concerns on the back burner. And for some mysterious reason, the closer it comes to the end of the day, food starts to become an issue. So let me ask you some questions. Who are you going home to? Who's coming home to you? Or, conversely, who isn't?

Why was my switch turned on at four o'clock, just about every day? Well, I was spent from the day with the kids. I wasn't involved in any activity then; we were usually home at this time. I was awaiting a husband who was coming home, and by now you've gotten our picture. Every time he walked through the door, he went to open the mail. And I went to open the fridge.

Once again, if the fire alarm is beeping every afternoon, you'll need to find out what's smoldering. What's going on at this time? Who is it going on with? Or is it the loneliest time of the day? By the way, that doesn't always mean solitude, as we can feel lonely surrounded by people.

I will tell you again that what you eat isn't nearly as crucial as the manner in which you eat it. When you let yourself go too long without food, once you get it you can't get enough. And you can't get it fast enough. I cannot begin to tell you how important it is, due to your current issues with food, that you keep hunger on a leash. Once it gets away from you it will be too hard to call it back. A snack for you is vital. Structuring it is even more so.

In the late afternoon, somewhere between three and four o'clock, I get terribly hungry. I used to try to wait for Scott to come home, which was never before seven o'clock. He wanted to play with the kids, who had already eaten. I was caught between my afternoon hunger at four o'clock, feeding my kids around six o'clock, trying not to eat, and waiting to eat at seven-thirty so I could enjoy a real dinner.

I ended up eating for the whole three hours in the form of picks, scraps, and an array of miscellaneous foods. It was never satisfying since I was trying *not* to eat. It wasn't filling because it was over a long period of time. And it was never "dinner," which I ended up skipping because I had eaten too much.

Structure. If I need to say it to you five hundred times I'll say it five hundred times. One of the reasons why I am successful in maintaining my weight is that I understand the importance of compartmentalizing my food. Breakfast, snack, lunch, snack, dinner, snack.

Obviously it is unrealistic to believe that every day is that regular. I will tell you when it's a must. When I am emotionally all over the place, structure is what will protect me. Never do I go a day without eating. Never do I skip lunch. *Never.* I know the danger in that. And besides, I love eating. Why would I skip that great meal?

In the late afternoon, you need to have something. Not too big, not too small, kind of Mama Bear–sized. Baby Bear is too small unless you had a late lunch. Papa Bear is okay, but consider that to be your early dinner and have a nice light snack later on. Very often, that's what I do since this is my hungry time. Do not approach dinner without having something to curb your hunger. Do not make the mistake of believing the less you eat here the better.

Think about what you are craving. Try not to open the cabinets and put the food in your mouth so impatiently. Give yourself a minute to think about what you want. Remember, this is not the easy time of the day. This is moving into the very toughest part. That brings me to another point.

This is not a bad time of the day to keep busy in an activity *in addition* to having that snack. Whether you're home with the kids or at work, keep yourself occupied. Don't do it to avoid eating the snack or you may overeat at dinner. Here are some snacks you could have and ones you can keep contained.

You could have apples in slices, but one apple isn't enough. Or maybe half of a cantaloupe. If you're at work you can bring all of these things from home. You could go to a coffee shop and try vanilla steamed milk or soy; did you listen to me yet and try it? How about hard-boiled eggs? If you eat only the white part, you can have ten of them. Dip them in some mustard; they're actually pretty good that way. You could have one of those protein bars; eat it with lots of water. I like oatmeal at this time. If you're at work, bring one of those flavored instant packets and microwave it. Fruit-and-yogurt smoothies are good; so is low-fat frozen yogurt.

My grandmother used to make me a snack that I make for myself and my kids. Now, this is not Nanny, this is Gramma. She also lived to the age of ninety-nine. Isn't that strange that both of my grandmothers died just short of one hundred? Genetically, this poses a problem. Can you imagine me having to live with myself for almost a hundred years? If other people get tired of me, at least they can leave. Where could I ever go?

Gramma was a vegetarian way before anyone else was. When my mom was a little girl she couldn't figure out why her milk was pink. It was because Gramma snuck carrot juice into it! Anyway, to make applesauce, she took a cut-up apple with the skin, a banana, a spoonful of honey, and four or five figs and put them in the blender. She would add maybe half a cup of apple, orange, or pineapple juice. You can use more if you like it thinner. It makes a very textured and sweet applesauce. You could make a meal out of it or eat half of it as a snack. Keep it in the fridge for a few days. It turns brown but tastes great. I should warn you, it looks a little like throw-up. Gramma's food was short on curb appeal, but healthy and high on taste.

You know what was so cool about Gramma? She was a pioneer in health. She used to feed me dulse, which is seaweed. I loved it. It's salty and delicious. You can buy it at any health-food store. If you like sushi, you're familiar with seaweed since it's used to make maki. Sea vegetables are full of vitamins and minerals that you won't get from other foods. There are many varieties, and if you soak them in water it will take out some of the salt. Use them in your salads or eat them plain as a snack. No kidding, they taste great, but they're ugly, like I said. Make sure you check your teeth before you smile too big. Gramma should have checked hers.

Here's another great blender snack. My kids love these, too, and they're very light but filling. Take a cup of skim milk or soy milk, five or six ice cubes, a very ripe banana (this makes good use of the brown ones that are overripe), and some frozen strawberries, blue-berries, or peaches. Add a couple of drops of vanilla extract. If it's for you and not for your kids, use some instant decaf and just a banana for a coffee-banana shake. You could use cocoa mix with the banana, too.

If I'm in the mood for bread, I'll have a couple of those small dinner rolls, the ones that are seventy calories. Sometimes I'll have some turkey. I do not ever have carrots or celery at this time. I am too hungry for that. Remember I mentioned heating cut-up apples in the microwave with cinnamon and light maple syrup? That's a perfect and satisfying snack. So is oatmeal with the apples. So is a waffle.

I stay away from foods that have no end. I try to keep structure here, too; no open bags of pretzels, where I can't keep track of what I've consumed. Not just in terms of calories; it simply feels more structured and will offer clarity to the amounts that you are eating. Your snack could be just about anything, but I wouldn't exceed two hundred calories. This is just to get you to dinner and cut the edge off your hunger.

Here are some more pointers as you're moving from snack to dinner. Do not cook dinner if you are starving. Have your snack before you begin cooking. If you want to eat your snack while you're cooking you can, but play around with that. You don't want that to spill over into a lot of tasting of the preparations. Make a mental choice not to eat a snack of the dinner you are preparing. Save dinner for dinner. Every bite you eat now is a bite less on your plate later on.

If you will be going out for dinner, your snack is very important. I have enough of a snack before we go so that I can hold out. But I do voice my preference for an earlier time and I'm no longer embarrassed to do that. I don't think that we need to feel ashamed of healthy choices that work for us. Or of letting people in on the fact that we get hungry earlier and it's hard to wait. Who cares? You think they don't have their issues? No one knows what goes on behind cabinet doors.

Chapter 42

*Y*our worst time is at night, right? You have a hard time staying out of the kitchen. I'll tell you what. Let's do dinner, and when we're done we'll curl up on the couch. There are some pretty important food discussions coming, but then I just want to talk. You know that's the part I like best. I feel like it keeps us connected.

What do you feel like having for dinner? If someone is making it for you, try to find out what it is so you know what to expect. Again, there is nothing wrong with being upfront about the fact that you're trying to plan your eating healthfully. If what they're serving sounds threatening to you, figure out why that is. Is it the person making it or the setting of where you'll be? Or is it food you don't feel safe with? Either way, you'll need to address that.

You may need, for now, to plan your own meals as you're learning what feels calm. You can also nicely offer to bring something that you will feel comfortable eating. Bring enough for everyone else, too. It is not insulting if the person knows you're trying to deal with a problem. As a matter of fact, it's admirable.

You want a balanced meal. You can choose at home, or anyplace else, to eat what you're comfortable eating. Whatever they are serving, if you keep it structured you won't have a problem. Here are some suggestions and guidelines, but your choices will need to be what works for you, not me.

Some sort of protein in the form of meat, chicken, fish, or eggs. For vegetarian options, try tofu, beans, or soy entrées. Cheese can be added in reasonable amounts to any of these for flavor, and it makes food more filling. I try to keep to one hundred calories with cheese that I add to my meals. If I want to go heavier on the cheese, I go lighter on the protein or dressing. You should have a vegetable and/or a salad. I often have protein of some sort and a big serving of vegetables and salad. I tend to stay away from bread and starches at dinner because I enjoy them more at lunch. Do not have a salad with a little chicken in it. Make sure you add a healthy portion of protein to fill you up.

You need a plate that is covered with food. Not those stupid, idiotic, pathetic teaspoonful servings that I see on dieters' plates. I also suggest dessert if it feels safe and you want one. There are many frozen low-fat desserts. What I like is that they're portioned out, so that helps you stick to structure.

Just make sure you eat. People look at me and don't believe I eat. I eat. I'm thin, and I didn't get there until I *started* eating. Get it? Not eating made me heavier. Eating made me thinner. Eat! I also can't stress enough the importance of eating things you like. The second you get tired of food that seems boring, you are ripe for a binge.

I'll tell you what I most often end up with in terms of timing as well as food. I no longer wait for Scott to eat if I'm feeling too hungry and he's late. Sorry. If I'm a bad wife because I don't eat when he eats then call me a bad wife. I was a worse wife when I overate, felt shitty, and got in a bad mood because of it.

As a matter of fact, sometimes I eat dinner at five o'clock. There are days when I want dinner food at 4:30 P.M. I no longer judge my hunger by the clock. Do I have to live on a farm to eat when the farmers eat? Should I let the clock tell me when I'm hungry? Fine, I'll set it ahead so I can eat my dinner in peace! If I'm hungry again later, I'll have some kind of light structured snack. I can eat that while Scott eats his dinner.

If we are nice to our spouses they won't care if we eat with them or not. If they care we need to make them understand our dilemma.

We need to let them know that we'll be making some changes in our eating habits, and that it's with an effort to make ourselves healthier and in better shape. Maybe they'll join us in that structure.

If you continue to have family issues, like a spouse who wants you to be on his or her schedule or children who come home later, you will need to have some discussions. There is nothing wrong with stating that you have tried to wait and it's causing you to overeat. Perhaps you can suggest some ways to compromise. Maybe there will be certain days designated when you all sit down together. Or maybe you all have such different time constraints that you will need to spend family time in other ways that do not revolve around food.

I believe it also sets an example to the kids that we need to eat when we're hungry. We may all be hungry at different times. We all need to compromise and adjust as much as possible. Let's find what works for us all as a family. And finally, you can say, "Right now I'm trying to figure out why I have been overeating. I'm learning to listen to my hunger and eat when my body tells me to. Please be patient with me as I work to understand my problem. And let me know if you have had problems, too. Maybe we can all learn together."

One more reminder here about the importance of a snack if you decide to eat dinner later. I establish my mood for food and I think about where we are going. If the place we're going has steaks or fish and that's what I'm in the mood for, then my snack will probably be fruit. I rarely have bread as a snack because I know I'll want to have some at the restaurant. If we are having pizza for dinner or something sort of starchy, my snack may be a Boca burger, turkey, or a protein bar. I won't want to overload on pizza, but I will want to eat a couple of slices. So I'll make sure I eat a snack.

To let you know what's coming, this is weekend talk. This was where I was with food beginning on Friday afternoon. This was *every* Friday afternoon. We'll go from structured healthy, which we already covered, to structured not so healthy. And just in case this should turn into a binge, we're going there as well. Put your seat belts on and just remember, it's only on paper.

Chapter 43

Friday night. Uh-oh. Friday through Sunday meant three to five pounds that were as automatic as a car wash. Weekends were anything but relaxing because the fear of food overwhelmed me. In retrospect, there were two things going on. There were emotions here, no doubt. But I also wanted a night off from healthy eating. I was ready for some weekend food. But I was so terrified of losing control that all I could do was fight it. Now I love Friday night. Whether it's during the weekend or any other day, let's learn to let ourselves go. As long as we let go with structure.

Junk Night should be fun. To make it less scary, again let's apply some logic. If you have been eating healthy foods in a structured manner, why can't Junk Night follow the same format? Let's walk through it from the beginning.

Let's say you are in the middle of cooking a dinner and you realize it's just not what you're in the mood for. You find yourself thinking about junk food or you're sampling snacks out of the cabinets. You know this feeling, right? You're going to try to catch yourself by simply changing the plan.

Give yourself a moment. What do you feel like tonight? And if the only answer you seem to come up with is cookies, ice cream, chips, and candy, wrap up the dinner you were supposed to have and begin to lay out your new food plan.

You need to constantly ask yourself the questions you would ask anyone else. What are you in the mood for? Do you want pizza, barbecue, or a burger with fries? Do you want a taco salad? Do you want a bowl of Frosted Flakes? Do you want a meal of snacks? And I'll ask you this question, too. Is it because of some feelings you're having or are you just in the mood for junk? Not sure? Here's the test.

Do you feel an uneasiness in your stomach, like an anxious kind of knot? Are you feeling a little racy, like you overdid the caffeine? Do you feel like you could cry or scream? Is there something going on in the next few hours or tomorrow that you don't want to do? Did you just finish something that made you feel uncomfortable? Someone you were with, something you did, or a phone call you had to make? Think.

We're going to deal with two answers. One answer is that this is not going to turn into a binge or some big emotional upheaval of food. You're just in the mood for cookies and ice cream or pizza with pepperoni. That's just fine. It's fun to eat that way sometimes and you cannot get fat from those foods, as long as you follow two rules. One is to let yourself have it, no matter what it is. The second rule is to stop yourself the moment your hunger is filled.

The reason why these new rules work and the old ones don't is that you get to have the fun. You get to have what you want. There are rules of safety attached to anything in life that holds danger. When you drive a car you wear a seat belt. When you ride a bike you wear a helmet. If you play football you wear protective gear. Would you deprive yourself of fun things that you love to do just because there's risk involved? Or would you just do them responsibly? Stopping when you're no longer hungry is the rule in the sport of Junk Night.

What we're looking for is balance. If you eat this way all the time, without the counter of light, healthy foods, then you can count on holding on to extra weight. If every time you open the refrigerator you dip into junk without any consciousness or structure, you will gain weight from that as well. What I'm suggesting is awareness, common sense, and the discipline not only of what you choose but of the structure you keep in check. Sometimes you have to say no and sometimes you get to say yes. The decisions are balanced by you.

If tonight's decision is junk food, here's how we do it. Decide what you want. For me, sometimes it's just snacks and desserts. Sometimes it's deep-dish pizza. Sometimes it's just a funky combination of several different foods. I do like the combination of sweet and salty, but I try not to go crazy with the salt; it makes me bloat up too much. I make very calculated, thoughtful decisions. Understand that, it's not like I'm conducting some survey with annual reports. I just give it some thought. It may take no more than a few seconds. The point is that there is thought. It's premeditated, not out of control.

When you eat junk because you are deciding to eat junk it feels different. It's not a "no," it's a "yes." It's not a bad thing; it's fun. There is no guilt since you are doing nothing wrong. It needn't make you anxious because you can still lose weight no matter what you're eating. It does not need to be endless because it won't be followed by deprivation. *You can have it again, any day you want it.*

You are making decisions about calories, too. Depending on what you had that day, and I'm assuming you had a reasonable amount of food, try keeping this to not much more than about five hundred calories. No matter what you had, that's not going to hurt you. If less is sufficient, eat less. If you ate lightly, have a bit more. If you are using the rule of hunger, though, more than five hundred calories would mean crossing the line.

Here's what I can buy with 500 calories. I might have 300 calories in cookies, 150 calories in ice cream, and if I want salty I'll have a few chips or Goldfish just for the taste. Or it could buy a couple of slices of pizza. If it's a burger and fries, I eat most of the burger and some of the fries. Then I go to my ritual. I take a chocolate calcium chew or finish with a piece of candy. If I'm home I brush my teeth. Done. Finito. The perfect end to the day.

This usually happens to me early. Sometimes as early as four o'clock, or a little bit later. How do I not eat again? It's easier than you think. That was my dinner. It was my choice because it was what I wanted. It was early because that's when my body told me it was hungry; I didn't just go by the clock. I bypass the dinner my family eats. I'm not that tempted by it either. I explain that I ate earlier because I was hungry. And certainly that is true.

With my kids, I allow them junk meals, too. Sometimes it's just what they want. If they have been eating terribly for days, I don't allow it. If they had junk at lunch, I insist on a healthier dinner. I encourage my kids to make choices for themselves, but I make them try healthy foods. I've been known to pay them to eat my vegetable soup. One nickel for spoonfuls that are small, a quarter if it's full of the vegetables. Oh, give me a break. Like you don't bribe your kids? At least it's for something positive, right?

If, after that early eating party I just had with myself, I find myself hungry a few hours later, I'll have an apple or some turkey or something not bready. Something not too substantial. I recommend you play it safe and stick to an apple or two. Then brush your teeth again. Why all this teeth brushing? I don't know; why do you wipe up the counter after every meal? Cleaning up is a ritual of finishing. So I clean up my teeth.

And I'll tell you another reason. In the past, I could never eat what I considered to be "bad" or fattening foods unless it was a part of overeating or bingeing. I mean never. So I keep myself safe with it even today. Whatever works for me works for me. What works for you will work for you. It's just allowing yourself what you want, and at the same time finding what works to keep you in line, safe from losing control.

That is the first answer to the question of where this is coming from. That first place being a mood having little to do with anxiety or those emotional forest fires. If this is a binge about to happen, and you're feeling out of control, let's now deal with that. I've got a new approach for you and it's got nothing to do with a bike ride.

Chapter 44

Binges come on like an earthquake. When you first feel the tremors you're never sure how severe it will be. Once it's over and the tremors are gone, you feel the destruction inside you. If you want to see how bad it was, you step on the Richter scale. You're a deep-feeling person, so you live close to the fault line. Quakes are common here. We're going to help you find the way to calm those tremors inside.

Those first moments are scary. This is as close to crazed as we get. Your heart starts racing, you don't want to do this, and there's just no way to stop it. I know how that feels. So as you approach that out-of-control place, just remember, I am right next to you and I'm holding your arm in my arm. We're going to stand through these moments together and calmly allow them to pass.

We have spent some time with structure. We know what we need to do there. But we're also not living in fairyland; binges are likely to happen. Remember, food mimics life and life is not fairyland either. Sometimes everything goes along fine and then spins out of control.

I want you to accept this moment. I know you don't want to. There are things in life you will need to accept even though you don't want to. This is happening. Today it's happening with food. One day it will be raging feelings and you'll need to get through those, too. The panic will feel exactly the same. But at least the food will be gone.

Look at this upcoming eating episode like a map with an arrow that says "You are here." This is where you are, and that just is what it is. Right now it doesn't matter why; you'll figure that out later if you haven't figured it out already. Right now we just need to get you through this.

On the top of the map is where you are going, the place you need to get to. We look at the map, which is your binge. We need to get you across in the most direct way possible. We don't want to walk around the long way; we want to cut right through to the destination point, that point being the end of the food.

You and I look at each other. We take a deep breath and accept that we just need to do this. We are not going to fight it or argue ourselves out of it. We are entitled to not be in control at all times. We are entitled to go crazy from time to time, and it may play out in our food. We are entitled to indulge in this moment. Next time we may not need to, but this is a time we do. So shoot us! We'll make sure our funeral's not on a Monday; we'd hate to have to miss it!

Accepting a binge will cut out half the food. You know why? Because you can be calmer in acceptance than you can be in the fight. Fighting something that's going to happen anyway takes a whole lot more energy than just going along with the current. Food mimics life here as well. Acceptance is the key to calm. You're going for the ride either way. That's a form of control, you know, just accepting what is.

What's our mood? Let's go back and forth if we have to. Bread? Sweets? Crunch? What does that little binge feel like? Be nice to it; it'll be nicer to you. It's a robber who's invaded our home. Give him the jewels and let him be on his way. This is about damage control. Got any funny jokes? I was kidding about the funeral; no one is dying here. We're gonna have some fun.

I used to eat huge quantities, as you know. Then I discovered a way to binge on lighter fare, and that's what I want to teach you. It's kind of like sample bingeing. I would take a few bites of a food I craved and then move on to another. I could have any food I wanted. Because I said yes and not no, the sample of each was enough. No more cereal boxes emptied. No more cookies out of control. I just got tastes of it all. And when I was done, I was fine.

I know your next question. How do I know when I'm done? Can I cut out a little early? Only if you want to come back. Let it run its course. You will know when you've had enough, but keep asking yourself the question in a nice and tolerant way. Don't be mad. Don't get frustrated with yourself. Take gentle care of this event so it won't spin out of control, and just ask yourself after each bite, "Have I had enough or is there something more I still want? What does my cute little self want now?"

Be prepared for the binges that are lunar. The ones where you feel possessed. The further along you go, the less often these will happen, but sometimes they still will. They still happen for me, too, sometimes, and they do not affect my weight. I just follow the rules I'll be showing you in the next chapter.

If this image helps you, I'm standing there with you. Maybe we're eating together or maybe you're eating alone. Either way, I am there. I am asking you if this food is making you feel better. I am asking you to make that decision. I want to make sure it's helping you. If it isn't, then maybe we'll end it.

If the answer is "Oh, yes, this really feels good and I'll stop in a little while," then I'll know not to interrupt you yet. If it's making you miserable, maybe you could stop here and have yourself a good cry or maybe you'll do that later. You might need to grieve in one of those healing "shivah" moments. You're having a reaction to something and you're feeling terrible inside. Maybe you can talk to me in your journal, just like I talk to you here. As soon as you're done with the food, it would be a good idea to do that.

This is the most horrible analogy, and you'll hate me for this, but I can't think of a better one to exhibit how you know when you're done. Well, you don't know how foul I can be; I've really been holding back. I'll warn you. If you are prone to motion sickness, have heart problems, or are pregnant, you may not want to read this. Here goes.

You know how you sit on the toilet to go number two? And there are those ones that could go a little longer and those that are over quickly? Well, if I were to ask you, "How do you know when you're finished?" you would give me the same answer I'll give you: You just know. And, if worse comes to worst, you get up to leave and you find you were somewhat mistaken; there's still a little more to go. So you simply resume your position. And you stay there until you're done. Pulitzer prize of analogies, don't you think? The food in the kitchen is the book by the toilet; you'll put it down when you're done. Pretty gruesome, huh? You're all right, just go splash some cold water on your face and put some ice on your temples.

After you are finished, forget it. It happened, it's over, move on. If you are someone who throws up after binges, this time you are not going to do that. That would be nonacceptance, and we're into acceptance now. This time you needed the food but you are learning other ways to cope. Give yourself that chance.

If you feel like throwing up the food you ate, go throw up your feelings instead. That means writing in your journal, or crying from your gut, just like we talked about earlier. That's what will make you feel better.

Once when I was in college, I tried to throw up my food. I tried so hard that I broke a blood vessel in my face. I never tried it again. While I can't relate to the actual behavior, I can relate to the feeling behind it.

If you are someone like I was, who would exercise after excessive eating to get rid of the calories, that is pointless, too. Exercising to compensate for any eating is the wrong reason to exercise. It's just as bad as throwing up. Exercise is for strength, energy, and stress busting, not to get rid of food.

Here is an amazing fact. I found that the day after heavy eating there are steps you can take that will give you a quick recovery. It's healthy, it's clean, it's honest, and it's accepting. And it's efficient in the long run in terms of losing your weight.

Remember, anytime you say no to the binge, you ask it to come back stronger. Anytime you beat yourself up, you'll not be able to get past it. You'll feel so bad about yourself that you'll cause yourself to eat again. All of this makes you gain weight. You've been caught in a weight-gaining cycle of eating and erasing, eating and erasing, whether you purged or worked out like crazy. I want you to try something new.

Chapter 45

Light, water, and wind. Not from the sun, not from the sea, but from the kitchen to the glass. And then to the source of your strength. The day after heavy eating, just eat light, drink a lot of water, and get your body in motion. I would prefer you not to exercise heavily because I know your motives in that. I don't want you "burning" off the food. I want you to burn the emotion. I want you to move through it with strength, and find your understanding.

Don't deprive yourself and don't stay away from food. That's what I used to do after binges. I would vow not to eat for a couple of days. I would run to do cardio, to make up those calories I consumed. Not eating made me hungry. The exercise made me hungry again and set me up to overeat. The more I told myself I couldn't eat since I had already eaten too much, the more I wanted that food. The more I made myself exercise, the more I felt entitled to eat. We're off that now because it simply doesn't work. Here's what does.

Have a light breakfast. Have maybe one hundred to two hundred calories and keep away from bread if you can. Start out the day with a great shower. Take a brisk walk or find a way to get yourself in a spirited form of movement. Not to burn the calories, I want you out of that cycle, but to reconnect with your core.

Lunchtime should be lighter today and snacks can be lighter, too. Try to have a light, healthy dinner of vegetables, fruit, and maybe a baked potato or some sort of protein you like. Yogurt, oatmeal, and eggs are light. Zone Perfect bars are good on these days. Just chug down water when you eat them.

If you are at work, this may be a good day not to go out to lunch if you can avoid it. If there is a lunch that you cannot get out of, order a light salad with some protein or have a bowl of soup. I don't recommend a sandwich today.

Let me tell you something. I rarely make lunch plans on Mondays. I know, most likely I will have eaten with less structure on the weekend. If I do go out, I make sure I am going somewhere that has safe food for me. I intentionally avoid places that have good bread baskets. As far as I've come does not mean I don't have to be careful. As far as I've come, it is awareness that keeps me safe.

If your calorie intake is somewhere between half and three-quarters of your daily average (the one suggested by a doctor or nutritionist), you'll get it off in the next day or two. Drink lots and lots of water. You'll flush out that food more quickly. Today is a day to eat, but try to take it easy. I don't want you hungry. I don't want you deprived. But you've eaten a lot of food recently and your system could use a light day.

It's important to feel healthy today, or as healthy as you can. You may not feel very well; that kind of eating makes us sick. Today you are recovering. Same as you would from having been sick. Yesterday, emotionally, you did feel sick, and now you need to make yourself better. Not with medicine or some kind of pill. Not from strenuous exercise either. Treat yourself as you would with a case of the flu. Eat very lightly and take it easy. Get back your strength so you can feel better fast.

It still baffles me, and I don't know if I'll ever get over the irony of this. I used to work so hard after a binge to try to reverse the process. Burn calories, deprive food, and sit out of my life. I put such extreme efforts into trying to erase the damage that would cause weight gain. I had no idea it could just happen on its own, without taking such ridiculously impossible measures.

Now I barely acknowledge it, other than to understand the feelings that set it off. It hardly ever happens. If it does it's so much smaller and less of an issue. I don't worry about it changing my body or putting me out of control. It doesn't change my body at all. It's nothing a light day won't fix. It doesn't change my life anymore; I would never give it that power.

What amazes me is that I lose whatever I put on faster if I allow myself to eat. Lightly as opposed to not at all. Light exercise without forcing myself to work out as much as I could stand. I think it's because I'm more relaxed about it now. If it happens I don't freak out. Taking the pressure off myself means I don't get set up for the cycle that puts me in a bad place again.

You may believe that the reason I don't get so upset about it anymore is because I am thin and can afford it. That simply isn't the case. There are people way thinner than I am who are terrified of a pound and horrified by the idea of overeating. I've been this thin in my life before and thought I was overweight. Thought I couldn't afford to eat. It's not my weight that allows this. It's me.

Not bad for an old bottom-of-the-box kind of girl, huh? Remember I asked why I didn't hate myself or hate my friend after we spent that day eating? The day we spent in her kitchen eating every imaginable food? What's to hate? I ate too much. I needed to at that time. But in the grand scheme of life it was pretty small potatoes. I'm not sure I mind that it happens occasionally in my life. I'd mind if I didn't understand it, or couldn't draw something from the event. It always tells me a story of something going on inside. And now it's told you one.

Chapter 46

My famous mentors, Doris and Goldie, walked into Melinda's office again. Sunny, fizzy, not quite as blond, but still the dynamic duo.

"I have the perfect life except for this one little problem." I went on to give some examples. "Anytime someone keeps me waiting or doesn't acknowledge my efforts, I start to feel angry inside. I feel like they don't appreciate me or feel a need to be with me. If they make anything or anyone more important than me, I act like a wounded child, and I become an irrational bitch. First I punish them by being cold. Then I don't let them in. In the moments this happens I can't see anything else and I can't seem to calm myself down.

"Sometimes it's even worse than that. Sometimes it feels like I am sick inside and there is something wrong with me. I get shaky and feel like my gut is hollow. I don't know what to do with myself. I need someone to make me feel better, but I don't know who to go to. In that moment there is no one. In that moment I am alone."

"Hmmm," says Melinda. As she brings her hand up to her chin, the thoughts mull around in her brain. She sees yachting trips and vacation homes, diamonds, furs, and tuitions. And that jacket at Neiman Marcus. This one will pay for it all. Issues of abandonment. A therapist's pension plan.

Situations have arisen that have caused me emotional upset. I know, I know, that's about as big a surprise as finding out cookies have sugar. What came as a loaded surprise, however, was an incredible realization. Situations are just like food; they mask what is underneath. I can blame circumstances for being the problem just like I used to blame food. Check this out:

What sits behind food is a feeling. It's not about the food. We just think it is, right? Likewise:

What sits behind situations are issues. It's not about the situation at all. We just think it is.

I gotta make sure you're getting this. I never got it before. A situation of life or a setup of circumstances can make us crazy. It can be something we just cannot handle. It makes us afraid. We lose control. We cannot be in that situation because of how it makes us feel. But here's the thing. It is *not* the situation that's the problem. We used to look at food and say the same words. We could not be around it. We could not control ourselves with it. It made us very afraid. And we knew, without a doubt, the problem was the food.

Food marks the spots where we have feelings, and we use those food cues as a red flag. Situations mark the spots of our issues, and that is the very same flag. It just goes one layer deeper. It brings up all those feelings again, forcing us to relive that pain. Remember Part Two of SAFE (Separate Always Feelings and Events).

Here's a light example. When someone leaves me to go on vacation, whether family or a friend, I get a terrible ache in my stomach like I may never see them again. This is a situation flagging an issue of mine. That panic I have marks an issue of my past. That one there is abandonment. Somewhere in my childhood, I had fears that were never dealt with. Now that I am an adult, rationally I can know certain things. But the child in me begs to differ. The child in me feels terror.

After I got married and had kids I assumed those feelings were gone. Guess what I found out? Those feelings are not gone at all! They are as there as when I was a kid. They come out when I find myself in situations that plug them back into the socket.

Often, it's not a situation that causes the pain to surface. Sometimes it rises from the absence of struggles; it happens when things become calm. That's when the feelings are given the luxury to stretch out their arms and reach us. It's that poke that sends us to food.

You want proof of that? People in deep grief, I mean deep, deep grief, usually lose their appetites. At the shivah house, it's the visitors eating the food, not the ones suffering the loss. When we receive very bad news, the shock takes away our hunger. In the event of the breakup of a relationship or the death of someone we love, often we seem to stop eating. Did anyone eat on 9/11? Wasn't the grief so all consuming that food on that day came second?

So when things are calm in our life, that's often when emotions heighten. Simply because they can. People in dire situations don't have time or ability to focus on food or what they're feeling. And people who are busy and occupied don't put their focus there, either. It's in the quiet times that we are able to indulge ourselves. This is an opportunity to roll up our sleeves and work, another Melinda phrase.

When seemingly light situations today trigger terrifying moments from my past, I'll need to walk myself through those moments just like I walk through a binge. I will need to structure my thoughts in the same way. I'll need to understand the source, far away from the current event, and understand they are just memories.

I feel the little girl inside of me whenever someone is leaving. I can cry and scream inside, just as I did long ago. Melinda has told me I need to talk to that child just like a mother would. Reassure her, from the adult in me, that everything is just fine. No one is really leaving me and I am not being left behind.

The only problem is that little girl is stubborn. She is very, very nasty. When I the adult try to talk to her, she is very hard to convince. Sometimes she is so hard to convince that she convinces me! I find myself seeing it her way!

This is why Melinda is now booking exotic vacations. She is meeting with architects and builders to add many wings to her home. This is why I have to hope that someday I will earn money. No husband could ever afford abandonment issues like mine without supplemental income.

Chapter 47

*Y*our car pulls into my driveway. You hear the gravel crunch under your tires. You step out of the car, approach my front door, and go to ring the bell. But there's a sign hanging on a nail:

GONE HOLING

The hole. What an awful place to visit. But what a safe retreat. When life gets too hard, and feelings get low, this is a place to hide. We disappear under our covers. Or we hide behind our job. We conceal the sick feeling we carry inside so no one knows it's there. We would love not to see anyone. We can't even talk about it. All we can do is hope it will pass. We have regressed again.

A typical stay in the hole can last anywhere from a few minutes to a hole lot longer. Another typo magnifico! I actually believe there's a huge and untapped market for a very lucrative business: hole decorating. We spend so much time in there. Why shouldn't we make it look pretty? Do you think we could get it holesale? Okay, I'll stop.

Then again, maybe I won't. You know how we look at everyone else and think they have it easier than we do? We look at their lives, we see what they show us, and we decide they are better off. The grass is always greener, right? Well, why don't you ask them for a tour? "Excuse me, mind if I have a look at your hole?"

It's possible they don't look inside their own hole; you know people try to stay out of there. But believe me, if they've gone down there, it ain't any better than ours. We all have a hole. And none of them is green! Fine. Now I'll stop.

A binge is the first step into the hole. The bigger the binge, or, for me today, the bigger the feeling and regression, the longer it takes to climb out. Melinda told me I could walk *around* the hole. I could have the feeling, know it's there, but choose not to go deep inside it. "I trip," I told her. "I tiptoe very carefully, but the smallest twig makes me lose my balance and then I can't help falling in." "Well," she says, "you could stumble around the hole and get back up, without falling in." Well, maybe *you* can. But maybe there are no trees where you live!

Melinda has helped me to identify my twigs. I know why these feelings trip me. But just like the days I couldn't stop eating, it's hard for me to walk away from the table of my feelings. When have I felt them enough? When can I be free of them?

I am trying to figure that out. But there is someone who offers me hope. She once had something she couldn't control, and she kept working and working and working at it. Finally she got past it. I am hoping that since I got past the food, I'll one day get past these feelings. In that sense, I'm my own inspiration.

I found that keeping busy and always making sure I have something to look forward to is like covering the hole with a board. Or like putting a ladder inside it. It doesn't mean that I won't have the feelings. It will just make "enough" come sooner. Here is a rung in my ladder.

Last night was Phyllis's sixty-fifth birthday party at my house. What a beautiful celebration. My dad came over early to make his special wild rice with Madeira wine and mushrooms. It took him three hours to prepare this one-hour dish. My dad poaches fish in the dishwasher. He cooks elaborate concoctions. He was about as emotional as a paper towel while I was growing up. And his cooking used to be awful. Now he's a cook and he's my girlfriend, and he's as emotional as they come.

This all came after I was an adult. It followed something painful that had happened in his life. He opened up. He needed me. The pain made him a very changed man. And that's when he met his Phyllis. Actually, she's my Phyllis. I picked her and it was long before she was pickable.

She had worked for my dad for years. They became very good friends over time. Whenever I'd go to his office, I would spend time talking to her. She was so warm and beautiful. Her skin was so soft and smooth. Every time she'd see me, she'd hug me. I remember telling her that since my dad couldn't be married to my mom, I wished it would be to her. This wasn't going to happen; Phyllis was married and had two children.

Many years later she told my dad she was getting divorced. When I heard about this I screamed, "Dad, don't you see what could happen here? If the chemistry works, this is it!" It did and it was. They were married several years later. The woman of my dreams for my dad.

At dinner last night I made a toast to the thirty people we were hosting. I said that one thing I often discuss with my friends is that there are two ways in which we give. One way is out of obligation or responsibility—something you have to do. The other way is from the heart, and tonight comes from my heart. Little did I know that wrapped in a beautiful red velvet box was a Baccarat crystal heart that Phyllis had bought for me.

Later, when I opened it, she told me why she had chosen it. "Because it comes from the heart. Every time you open this," she said, "hold it in your hand. It's smooth and feels good in your palm. And whenever you're feeling bad, just hold it and feel me holding you." See why I picked this woman?

Last night was one of those perfect moments in life. Everything that was happening was so genuine to what we all felt. I loved seeing my dad so happy. And so in love with his wife. Only love like that could drive a man to spend three hours cooking rice. He overprovided in mushrooms. He confessed to me later that he got so tired of cutting all those mushrooms that he began to throw them in whole. He figured people could cut their own damn mushrooms; his fingers were falling off.

We cooked, we laughed, and we talked about how great he is. My dad loves to talk about that. We all put up with that for two very good reasons. One is how much he enjoys the subject. The other is that he's right. My stories about my dad are so telling of his never-ending sense of fun. Once in college, I called him to say, "Dad, I've got good news and bad news. Which one do you want to hear first?" He told me he wanted the good news first, so I told him. "Now for the bad news," I said. Click went the phone. Real funny, Dad.

Then there was the time my dad took my sister and me away for the weekend. I had gotten my first period that week and thought it had ended. When it came back, I asked my dad why that had happened. "That's because it wasn't really a period," he said. "It was really just a comma."

My dad had a thing about running out of gas all the time. Once when he was driving with Nanny, he ran out on the highway. Since it was pouring that day she gave him her plastic rain hat. You know, the kind that all grandmas wear with the strings that tie under the chin. She sat in the car by herself while he walked to the nearest station.

Apparently there had been a chain-link fence he had had to climb, and he tore his pants wide open. Finally he saw a car and tapped on the man's window for help. The man took one look at that Saran wrap hat and flew the heck out of there. By the time he returned back to Nanny, the police had moved her elsewhere.

He decided to get smart, though. How? You're probably assuming he filled up the tank when he got down to a quarter, but you'd be forgetting that this is my dad. He bought a folding bicycle to keep in his car so he could get to the station more quickly. Then Nanny wouldn't have to wait so long and the cops wouldn't have to move her.

Not all dads go to aerobic classes with their daughters either. One might not have noticed his complete lack of rhythm and coordination had he at least gone in the same direction as the rest of the class. But no, no, not my dad. He had to go the opposite way. Arms flailing around him, his body moving side to side while all the other bodies moved front to back. His hands were held palms facing out as he skated across the room, bumping into everyone in his way. Totally unaware. And so proud of himself, too. I watched him in utter amazement, my mouth hanging open as he moved about in all of his glory.

My dad is an example of what happens at the intersection of pain, need, and fun. He has gone through some very painful times. He is needy of attention and stroking. To the point that it's quite intolerable. But he has more spirit and life than six squads of pom-pom girls cheering on their winning teams. It's with that same level of enthusiasm that he cheers on the people he loves. In everything they do. It's why we all love him so much.

And he's right about something else. It's all about the story. He would laugh and tell us, "If I didn't do all those things, what would you have to talk about?" I'll take that one step further, one step beyond my fabulous father. Without my eating issues, my painful past, and my horrible nightmares with food, what would have been my story? Where would I be in this moment?

How can I not be grateful for whatever brought me here? The largeness of my dad's message is so much larger than I ever knew. I could begrudge the food and my past, but without it I wouldn't be where I am right now. I wouldn't have had these discoveries. The food was the flashlight that helped me see in the dark; it led me to myself. And then brought me here to you. My story is what brought us together. So I will no longer see an event of eating as a bad thing in my life. I just keep that bicycle folded up in my head, and ride to the understanding.

Chapter 48

"*Mom, when are we going to be there?*" Soon. Very soon. As soon as we drive the point home.

We are almost finished, but I am concerned about something. I am concerned that you still look at me and say, "That is her, not me." Just like I looked at other people and said it was them and not me. Then I went to the diets again. I don't need to go on here, do I?

You need to listen to what I'm telling you. You need to hear it and believe me. Eating does not make you fat. Monsters don't live in the closet and food is not your enemy. It isn't about the food or the weight or what number is on that scale. Those are the places you direct your fear. But fearing food is not rational. That's why it doesn't make sense. When you ask how someone could be controlled by a cookie, or by a bowl of potato chips, you admit it just doesn't fit. What you're not seeing is why you do it.

It's because you are scared of life. Not food. You are afraid of those feelings that hurt you and others. Not of what's on the scale. To believe you have no control is very true. You have no control over some things in life. But over a lot of it you do. Next time you look at an event of food and say you have no control, stop and look at that same event and find out where you do.

Life is scary stuff. So many bad things can happen. Your fear is of that. Your fear is that you won't be able to handle it if it does. Your fear is that the people around you won't be able to either. You think that if you're strong enough to live without food or at least control what it does, you will be able to control the rest. But you can't. Nor can you control what you feel. You're not supposed to control that. It's a part of your life and who you are. Feel it and live it. That's the gift that you were given the second you took your first breath.

What is the real fear? Not the irrational fear that you can't stop eating or that food can somehow take over. It's of the events that just happen when there's nothing we can do to stop them. The potato chip isn't scary. The potato chip has no consequence. Life's events are scary and they have dramatic and altering consequences. But that's all right. You've lived this long and survived every single one of them.

Don't be afraid of the truth. Don't be afraid of what's happened, what hasn't happened, what may never happen, or what may still happen. Don't be afraid of what you've done, what you haven't done, or what you may or may never do. There is one thing so much worse than all of your fears put together. And that is the life you could be living if you weren't so stuck in the food.

These are words I hear you use when you describe what food brings to you: Happiness. Something to look forward to. Feeling good. Feeling excited. Something to think about. Something to control. Something to occupy your time. Something to do with your hands. Something to share with others. If it had nothing to do with hunger, you would never live without it. Life would be empty without food.

There's a whole world waiting for you and your talents, for you and your mind, for you and your accomplishments, and all you have to give. As you put all of that energy and dedication to diet and food, your life is passing you by. The clock is ticking and you think it's to lunch. It ticks to your life being wasted. As you continue to make food your life.

I don't care what it is. I don't care how you find it. Whether it lasts a day, a week, or forever. Take a piece of life that you haven't tried before. You've been depriving yourself way too long. You must be so starving and bored. Go pile up large plates of it and sample it all around. Never say no, there's no such thing as too much. When it comes to life you can binge; it will never make you gain weight.

Run down those aisles, look at the choices: pottery classes, rock climbing, photography. Take a writing course, take an acting class, or learn to play the guitar. Go hold newborns in intensive care, or visit the elderly and make them smile. Make the person in the toll booth laugh. Talk to the person who works a counter. Work a campaign, head a program at school, start swimming, or take up tennis. Get a job, or create something new in the job that you already have. Make a few new friends. Make this huge world smaller, by connecting some of the dots. You say you don't have time? Yes, you do. You have the rest of your life.

Chapter 49

She never wore the same clothes twice. She wore this wonderful perfume. I would stay after school and talk to her. I even gave her my journals to read. She must have sensed my reaching out to her and she responded to me in kind. I was twelve years old. She had just turned twenty. Miss Colby was my student teacher.

She would drive me home sometimes. It felt like hitching a ride with a star. She was the first person in my life who made me feel like I stood out. After all, here she was with *me*. I wanted to be her little sister. I wanted to be her friend. I wanted to be . . . *her*. She was getting married to the most handsome man I had ever seen. His bright blue car had a white interior. They were such a beautiful couple. But I had some sad news to face.

They were moving to Atlanta and I wouldn't be seeing her anymore. She told me we would write. Famous last words, right? Wrong. She may have moved away, but it only brought us closer. The only thing dropped was her teacher's name. She became my dear friend Abby.

We have had more than thirty years of friendship. We have watched each other grow up. The eight years don't make such a difference anymore, but she still likes to be my teacher. And that's just fine with me.

Abby is a brilliant pursuer of life. She ran a marathon but she didn't stop at one. She stopped somewhere around thirty-seven and got her husband running nearly half as many. Every goal she sets she exceeds. I never had such goals.

My friend Debbie and I had been running along the lake almost every day and she had this idea we should train for a marathon. Hours of running, hours of talking; we shared every piece of our lives. We chose a marathon in Houston since the timing of it matched our training schedule. The night before we were to go, I came down with a fever and the doctor said I could not run it. Debbie flew out there and finished it. I stayed home and cried.

I had been so proud to talk about it during our training. I wouldn't be just someone's wife or mother, I could be someone who did something big. This was so typical of goals in my life; just one more thing unfinished.

Scott came to my rescue. I felt like he picked up my broken bike and found a way to fix it. He told me to find another marathon anywhere in the country, and we would fly there together. Long Beach, California, had one three weeks later.

When Abby heard what had happened, she felt terrible for me. She knew I was nervous to run it alone. She wanted to come and meet me there and run the marathon with me. I told her how much I loved her thought, but I wanted to do this alone. She insisted on coming anyway, but I was torn about her decision. So she promised I would run it alone.

Finishing a marathon is a physical impossibility. Why would someone's body be able to run 26.2 miles? Abby and I started out running together. Later I wanted to pick up speed and she encouraged me to run ahead. Scott was on Rollerblades, meeting me at various points. I always had him to look forward to; he showed up at the perfect times.

Around the twenty-second mile, I began to hurt. It was getting harder and harder to run. I wanted to stop and I started to cry. I just couldn't finish this. Scott was always ahead. Abby was staying behind. I couldn't imagine ever finishing. But I couldn't let myself stop.

My legs felt like they were no longer attached. I knew my body was moving forward in some sort of dragging run. Scott would now appear at each of the mile markers, and continued to cheer me on. The twenty-sixth marker had come. There was still the two-tenths to go. This was such an unreasonable goal. Why couldn't it be just twenty-six?

Up ahead I could see the balloons. The band, the crowd, and the clocks. I could see the sign that said FINISH. I felt a rush and a flow of tears. I crossed the line and read my time. It was 4:07, seven minutes past my goal. My second goal, since my first one was just to finish. And once I had stopped I had this incredible realization; I couldn't even stand up! Abby came in sometime after, having watched me the whole way through. Knowing she was behind me helped me keep my pace. Once again, I had hitched a ride from a star.

It was the first time I set a plan and stuck to it. It was the first time I didn't let a setback stop me from going ahead. And it was the first time I followed my instinct of the way I needed to do this, even though it meant turning down the loving intentions of my friend.

I have no desire to run another marathon, but I will never forget that high. It was the day I knew I could do anything. It was the first thing I had ever finished; you know, besides my plate. Today I run really fast, about a 7.20-minute mile. Not to burn calories or burn off food; just to show myself I can do it. It was just another redefined challenge.

The other day I was on a bike ride with my beautiful "baby boy." He had set himself a goal. He wanted to go all the way to the end of the route we ride along the lake. Down to the beach stop 1. I told him that was such a long way and we didn't have to go so far. He insisted we did and counted down as we rode.

When we finally got there, I made him get off the bike and I had him touch the pole of the sign. The sign that said 1. He asked me why he had to touch it. I told him about goals and the importance of having them in our lives. I wanted him to feel proud of the goal he had just reached. I wanted him to touch it.

This was my tribute to Debbie. She was the one who taught me to touch that pole. There was a time I could barely run a mile; I would pant and nearly fall over. There was a time I was told not to have a third child, and that I'd be foolish to take that chance. But I went on to cross the finish line, the first goal I set and completed. And then was a part of an even better goal, the one I would share with this child. There is just no such thing as *can't*. In a world of *just believe*.

Chapter 50

I've got another surprise for you. I exercise far less than I did years ago. My body is stronger. My weight is lower. And I am ten years older. How's that for some great news, huh?

Here's how I see it. Rail-skinny, nonathletic bodies are no longer attractive to me. I don't see "thin," I see problems. I see someone who doesn't eat. I don't like huge muscles either; I see obsessions in that as well. I like what I see in Hollywood now; for the first time there's more of a range. People are regarded as beautiful who aren't skinny and looking unfed.

I used to think if I missed a day of working out, my body would lose its muscle. The food would make me gain weight if I didn't cancel it out with a run. I couldn't let myself take a break.

Today, I still work out. I do my core training twice a week with Mark. I'll walk or take a cardio circuit class with another great trainer named Laura. Or sometimes I'll play tennis. If I miss a couple of days it doesn't change my weight. It just changes the way I feel.

I would like to address those of you who just can't get into it. You hate it, you're not interested, and when you've tried it you've given up. Can I ask you to try again, but with a totally different mind-set?

Take a walk, even if it's just around the block. I want you to try to get moving. Tap into that core. Take note of all the working parts; notice what you feel. See that when you move your arms, it makes your body go faster. Notice that when you take long strides, you feel muscles respond right away. Suck in your gut, stand up straight; feel taller and leaner and stronger. You're breathing harder, imagine that. It must mean you're really alive.

Try some tips from Laura's class. Everything we do is in three-minute intervals. She'll have us run, walk, throw a med ball against a wall, combine jumping jacks with sprints, and perform a variety of other moves. Find a program like Laura's. Or make up one on your own. Run to the first stop sign and then walk to the next one. The three-minute theory works. In your mind, whatever you're doing ends in just a couple of minutes. The changes make the time go fast.

This is not to lose weight. This is just to feel you. This is learning the potential strength that your body's had all along. No matter how old you are or what you think of yourself, you could be better than you are today. Better means better use. Better progress toward showing yourself what you've got and how you're willing to care for it. You are going to amaze yourself, and see what good health feels like.

Muscles are magnificent. Strength is so full of vigor. Feeling your body's power is the most amazing feat to behold. It's truly a natural joy and a high that is complete and fulfilling. Don't make your body a victim that whispers inability and weakness. Let your body scream action and drive. Let it run you all the way home.

Chapter 51

My sister says I repeat myself and it really gets annoying. My sister says I repeat myself and it really gets annoying. I can't help it! You know how I need to be heard. What if someone missed my point? What if I just want to keep you here and I can't ever let you go?

Before I start getting emotional about it, let's go over what we've talked about so I know you've got a plan. The closer you stick to the plan, the closer we stay together. It keeps us on the same page. Stay close, you promise? In my heart we're connected for life. And don't you ever forget it. Here we go:

The journals. Remember, one notebook is all about food. The other one is about what you're feeling. Your food journal tells you how you eat. Write down every bite, every pick, and everything you put in your mouth. Notice patterns with times of day and activities that surround them.

This notebook will point out whether you eat with structure. It logs the time of day when eating gets out of control. By looking back at the pages, you will be able to see patterns of that. Use a small notebook that you can carry around easily. Put it in a purse or a briefcase. Keep it in the car if you need to. I can't tell you how important this is.

Your second notebook doesn't need to be with you all the time;

you can just write in it at home. I will tell you, however, that when you find yourself waiting someplace, writing in your journal is a wonderful use of that time. Also, if you're somewhere and you begin to feel those tremors, it may help to disappear for a few moments and talk to your journal, as though you were talking to me, or a therapist, or a trusted friend.

The most effective way to use both of your journals is not only to record your food in one and your thoughts in the other but to cross-reference between the two. Remember my Sundays? If I had not seen the pattern of my eating and where I was at the time, I would never have solved the issues.

If you refuse to monitor your food, there is a reason why you need crazy food. You're not willing to give up this cycle. What's it doing for you? What's it keeping you from? Ask yourself over and over, what would it be like without it?

The alarm system. A food thought is a beep. It's information on the keypad that something is stirring inside. Figure out what it is and find the choice that will disarm the beep.

SAFE (Separate Always Food and Emotion). Whenever you hear that beep, ask yourself what's going on. Whatever it is, deal with it away from the food, unless of course it's hunger. If it is, then eat something you'll enjoy. Use common sense but feed your cravings. If, on the other hand, it's a person or situation causing this response, figure out what it is and find your choices within. Food isn't the problem. But it will be until you find out what is.

Sitting with feelings. Food is used to distract us from the feelings we don't want to face. Run through some of the emotions you may be experiencing. Are you feeling angry? Sit with it and steam. Do you need to express that anger? Write about it in your journal. If you need to have a conversation with someone, consider exercising *before* you do that. It will take the bite out of your anger and allow you to talk from a rational place. Is the emotion loneliness, sadness, or depression? Is this a feeling from your past? Feel it and go as deep as you can. Maybe you'll get lucky and start crying. Getting it out is healing.

Choices. Once we identify the feelings in any given situation or moment, we are presented with a choice. Making this choice, small or large, is what ultimately frees us from food. The choice may be acceptance of something that's not going to change. Or the choice may require a change. Either way it's a choice. Make it or keep fighting food.

SAFE Part Two (Separate Always Feelings and Events). One person could go crazy when someone they're meeting is late. Another person couldn't care less. It's not the "lateness" that's the issue here. It's the feeling behind the event. What does it make you feel? What memory does it trigger? Pull it at the root.

Goals. Make sure that losing weight is not your only goal. Begin to add small goals, and I do mean small. Do not set yourself up for disappointment by thinking it has to be huge. Small projects in your home or even in your community are wonderful places to start. A goal in fitness is a good one, too, but don't make it about losing weight, right? Let weight loss be the by-product of a life that's full and rewarding.

Eat! It is the only way to lose weight. Deprivation and restriction will lead to overeating. Allow yourself foods that you enjoy on a normal basis, with a balance of healthy foods and the allowance of treats as well.

Structure. When all else fails, this is your rescue squad. Three meals, three snacks, and don't ever miss a meal. Balance 85 percent healthy and give yourself 15 percent in fun treats. Any food is fair game. Attempt to eat until you're satisfied, which is a different feeling than full.

Binges. You will treat them like a robber who has invaded your home. You will calmly ask the binge what he wants. You will give him exactly what he asks for. Offer him variety and don't let him spend too much time on one food. The more he sees and tastes, the less he will take overall.

The day after a binge. Eat lightly but eat. Drink lots of water. Get some movement in your day with some sort of exercise, but not to burn off the food, just to put energy back in the right place.

Exercise. Not to burn calories and not to lose weight. You want to feel your core and tap into energy and strength. Try walking as fast as you can, or run as fast as you can. Sprint the walk or run for two minutes and then slow down for one minute. Repeat the patterns and create new ones. Open the door of the stall and let that horse break free.

Redirecting energy. The pain may always be there. Facing it may not make it feel any better. As a matter of fact, it may feel even worse. *After* you have faced it and felt it, and then you have felt it some more, you'll come to a place where you're done being miserable. You will find something to pour yourself into. It is here that purpose meets drive. It is here that passion is born. This is the county line that separates Kansas and Oz.

Cross it.

Epilogue

I laid them all on the bed. My obsessions, my resentments, my panics, my anger, my hurt, and all of my blaming. I lifted them carefully so as not to lose any particles of them. I placed them in the thick, heavy bag and sealed the bag up tight. I made sure there was no opening anywhere; I didn't want to waste an ounce. I shook the bag as hard as I could. I stomped on it, kneaded it, and ground it down until all that was there was a powder.

I recalled all the pictures and memories of what had made them so large in my life. None of that would matter anymore; their strength was needed elsewhere. I sat down and began to write. All of the energy from that bag was pushing my fingers to type. One thought, one word, one press to the keyboard. One speck at a time.

I do remember a line written down early on in those pages. It was about energy and obsessions and all they steal from life. "Imagine that strength redirected," it read. "Holy smokes. Imagine that strength redirected."

Imagine.

The Last Page

The camp buses are all lined up. The motors have all been running. You can hear that oh-so-familiar *whoosh* of the doors as they open and close. The camp seems so barren and burned, as if it knows not to look green anymore. The duffels are packed, the cabins are empty, and it's time for us to go home. I can't believe that day has come. I'm not ready to say good-bye.

Wow. What can I possibly say? You read me, you heard me, you listened to me. You stayed with me all of this time. *You never abandoned me!* Well, I won't abandon you, either.

I've known all along that we would come to this place and I knew it would feel like an ending. As I felt its approach, I so badly wanted to stall and draw out the time. Back at page one I had no idea where this was going. Here, at The Last Page, I know.

My gosh. You've seen the most personal and intimate parts of who I am. And while I couldn't hear your response, I absolutely felt you there. I felt your support, I felt your caring, and I imagined you nodding your head. I knew when I got a laugh or a smile and I knew when you felt sad with me. We shared something here, I could feel it. And that's something I'll never let go of.

As I've prepared myself for the release of this book, you'll never believe what's happened. It's made me crazy. No, I mean *more* crazy! I got me some nice little attacks of the sweats. Thought I was in menopause! You know what's so funny? If I didn't have issues, I wouldn't be here, right? I never would have written this book. But can a girl with issues handle the anxiety of exposing her innermost? Well, I'll be sure to let you know.

I feel so nostalgic, like I want to reminisce. Remember that page where we first met? We didn't know we would be friends? We thought this would be a way for you to lose weight and a way for me to help you get there. Remember when I didn't even know your name? Remember that I still don't? Oh, I am going to miss you.

You made a commitment by staying here. By going deeper, I made one, too. Now we need to trade roles. I need to stay and wait with you now. And you need to somehow go deeper. As soon as you live honest and true to who you are inside and never stray from yourself, you'll enjoy better health. And you'll live and feel life more deeply. Don't you ever stop fighting for your voice, you hear? I want you to make sure you're heard. You are strong enough for that, and so are those around you.

I guess we both have our work. We need to walk through issues again and again, and get better and stronger each time. We know they don't go away. We know they sneak up all the time. But we're also learning how capable we are of changing how we handle those moments. I'm proud of us, aren't you?

I hope and pray for your happiness. I want you to watch for your health. Don't forget what I said at the very beginning, about that food energy redirected. If this didn't prove it then nothing will, since writing to you has come from that place.

Promise me you'll write in your journals. And promise me you will have fun. Let's leave off with a comma, so we know that it's never good-bye. I don't know when, I won't know how, and I suppose neither do you. Just hold on tight and never let go. I won't let go, either. That way we'll be together, my friend, in some form of our connection. Long after the words

The End,

Acknowledgments

I dedicate this book to my husband, Scott. To read the name of the author is to understand my thanks. You gave me a place to be Nancy Goodman. You brought me to a place that was safe and warm and cozy. I never had to worry about feeling homeless inside, since you always provided that security.

I often complained that you set no boundaries. You let me go too far with my anger and behavior, and my talk of letting go. But because you set no boundaries, while providing the safety of our home, you allowed me to run free and crazy, to find freedom from my demons and fears.

You have been my best buddy. My partner. My family. You have taught me about goodness, solidity, selflessness, and the importance of being a good guy. You made me Mom to the most beautiful faces I have ever seen. Wherever life takes us, wherever we go, I'll stay right behind you, too. You have that place in my heart that is as strong as the homes you provide. We once moved a house and set it in another spot. The house can go wherever it wants, but the feelings won't leave their foundation. Some things just stay unmovable. I love you that much and more.

Thank you for reading every page, even when you were tired; for your thoughts, your interest, and praise; for the pain it caused in the words that were there and the pain in the words that were not; for believing in me and staying with me when I made it so hard to be there. And thank you for not filling my car with oil. Why in the world should you?

There's no doubt in my mind why we picked our wedding song, "Something Good," from the musical *The Sound of Music*. The title of the song carries the words of the theme we live by. "Perhaps I had a wicked childhood/Perhaps I had a miserable youth/But somewhere in my wicked, miserable past/There must have been a moment of truth./For here you are, standing there, loving me/Whether or not you should/So somewhere in my youth or childhood/I must have done something . . ./Soooome thiiiing goooood."

There is a Jimmy Stewart movie we all know with an unconventional angel. He shows George Bailey what the world would have been like if he had never been born. In my life there was an unconventional angel as well, and she had the name of Melinda. I was given a gift by Melinda, similar to George's. To see what life can really be like when you take the truth and face it. And find the true you inside. And just like George, with tears in his eyes, after all was said and done, after deep sadness and fear and some terrible days, he could stand back and finally say, "It's a wonderful life."

To Lani, Sam, and Alex, if you could have whatever you wanted I know what it would include: a personal shopper for Lani, a Hummer H1 for Sam, and Alex wants bugs and crystal. But let me tell you what my wish is for you. Outside of the big ones—good health, safety, and happiness—I wish you something else. I wish you the strength to trust in your instincts.

Don't ever argue with feelings. They are a part of your nature and part of what makes you unique. If you study and understand them, they will give you all of your clues. They will tell you all about you, and the more you know the better.

I know you're strong because you're loved. You're safe because you're strong. You are three of the most incredible people I know. As you grow older and have new beginnings, your lives will be full of changes. And changes are so scary at times. But always recall the changes you've made already, in your very young years so far. However scary they seemed at the time, and, boy oh boy, did they ever, you moved on quickly to find that it really wasn't so bad. And you even found life to be better. As long as you keep your flexibility, you'll always make the stretch.

I love you. I inhale you. I apologize for loving the smell of your feet. I want to stick my nose in your necks, and breathe as far as my breath can go. I know you hate when I smell you, but what you have to understand is that nothing in this world smells better than the deepest form of love. It's the sweetest smell on earth. Especially while you sleep.

Thanks for being mine. Thanks for calling me Mom. Thanks for making fun of me and making me feel so stupid! And thanks for giving me hiccups from laughing so hard and fast. My babies. There is nothing more precious than you.

This book is full of dedications to those I want to thank. But when it comes to the miracles of my life, your faces are what I see. Lani. Sammy. Alex. The ones who make scents of my life.

There was a woman sitting on the side of the river. In her lap was a book she had written. She needed to get the book up the river, but she had no way to get there. She kept calling out to the passing boats. "Please take me up the river," she pleaded. "I need to get my book to the people who live there."

Just as she was about to give up, a tall, gentle-faced man with a beard stopped to talk to her on the riverbank. He told her he believed her book would help a lot of people. "You mean you'll take me on your boat?" she cried. He told her he would. He promised he would do his best to find someone to carry them farther. The man's name was Ned Leavitt from the Ned Leavitt Agency. And he had a crew member by the name of Britta. A man named David Smith had told Ned where the woman was waiting.

Ned and Britta took the woman in their boat and headed up the river. They knew she had never been on a boat before and they were patient and kind to her. They did everything possible to make her comfortable for the journey that lay ahead.

Ned asked many boats along the way if they could get this book to the people. But one boat was a ship, a Viking ship, with a Penguin in the galley. The woman driving this mighty ship was named Janet Goldstein.

Janet went back to her Viking crew. They all believed in the message and decided it was worth the trip. Janet not only protected the book, she found a way to make it stronger. By reaching inside the written words, she helped the woman find more. They sailed smoothly together, and the book reached its destination.

Ned Leavitt and Janet Goldstein. The sailors behind her dream.

To Veronica Murtagh
   It was my title vs. your title, and your title won!

And finally...

You delivered all of my babies.
You gave us hope when others did not.
You gave us the courage to have that third child
and you directed me to Melinda.

You have seen me through so many beginnings
I just had to save your name for last.
Dr. Randall Toig.